First World War
and Army of Occupation
War Diary
France, Belgium and Germany

21 DIVISION
Divisional Troops
38 Sanitary Section
11 September 1915 - 31 March 1917

WO95/2148/3

The Naval & Military Press Ltd
www.nmarchive.com
Published in association with The National Archives

Published by

The Naval & Military Press Ltd

Unit 10 Ridgewood Industrial Park,

Uckfield, East Sussex,

TN22 5QE England

Tel: +44 (0) 1825 749494

www.naval-military-press.com

www.nmarchive.com

This diary has been reprinted in facsimile from the original. Any imperfections are inevitably reproduced and the quality may fall short of modern type and cartographic standards.

© Crown Copyright
Images reproduced by permission of The National Archives, London, England, 2015.

Contents

Document type	Place/Title	Date From	Date To
Heading	WO95/2148/3 38 Sanitary Section		
Heading	21st Division 38th Sanitary Section Sep 1915-1917 Mar To 3 Army		
Heading	21st Division 21st Divisional Sanitary Sect. (no 38) Vol I Sept 15		
War Diary	Milford	11/09/1915	11/09/1915
War Diary	Havre	12/09/1915	12/09/1915
War Diary	Audruieque	13/09/1915	13/09/1915
War Diary	Watten	13/09/1915	22/09/1915
War Diary	Magniyade	23/09/1915	24/09/1915
War Diary	Noeux Les Mines	24/09/1915	24/09/1915
War Diary	La Philmphe	24/09/1915	30/09/1915
Heading	21st Division 38th Sanitary Section 21st Div Vol 2 Oct 15		
War Diary	Morbeque	01/10/1915	01/10/1915
War Diary	Hondeghem	02/10/1915	02/10/1915
War Diary	Menirs	06/10/1915	31/10/1915
Heading	21 Div 38th Sany Section Vol 4		
Heading	War Diary Of O/C N 38 Sanitary Section 21st Division From 1st Dec 1915 To 31st Dec 1915		
War Diary	Field	01/12/1915	31/12/1915
Heading	21st Div 38th San Sect Vol 5 Jan 16		
Heading	War Diary Of No 38 Sanitary Section From 1st To 31st January 1916		
War Diary	Armentieres	01/01/1916	31/01/1916
Heading	No 38 Sanitary Section Feb 1916		
Heading	War Diary Of No 38 Sanitary Section From 1st February Till 29th Feby 1916		
War Diary	Armentieres	01/02/1916	29/02/1916
Heading	War Diary Of No 38 Sanitary Section From 1st March 1916 Till 31st March 1916 Vol 7		
War Diary	Armentieres	01/03/1916	22/03/1916
War Diary	Merris	23/03/1916	31/03/1916
Heading	War Diary Of 38th Sanitary Section 21st Divisional Sanitary Section For April 1916		
War Diary	Merris	01/04/1916	01/04/1916
War Diary	Ribemont	02/04/1916	30/04/1916
Heading	War Diary For May 1916 Vol 9		
War Diary	Field	01/05/1916	22/05/1916
War Diary	Ribemont	23/05/1916	31/05/1916
Heading	War Diary Of No 38 Sanitary Section For June 1916 Vol 10		
War Diary	Ribemont	01/06/1916	30/06/1916
Heading	21st Divn 38th Sany Section July 1916		
War Diary	Ribemont	01/07/1916	04/07/1916
War Diary	Belloy-Sur-Somme	05/07/1916	07/07/1916
War Diary	Cavillon	08/07/1916	10/07/1916
War Diary	Ville Sur Ancre	11/07/1916	20/07/1916
War Diary	Cavillon	21/07/1916	23/07/1916
War Diary	Le Cauroy	24/07/1916	30/07/1916

War Diary	Duisans	31/07/1916	31/07/1916
Heading	War Diary For August 1916 21st Div 38th San Sect Vol 12		
War Diary	Duisans	01/08/1916	31/08/1916
Heading	21st Div 38th Sanitary Section Sept 1916		
War Diary	Duisans	01/09/1916	05/09/1916
War Diary	Le Cauroy	06/09/1916	12/09/1916
War Diary	Le Cauroy Buire	13/09/1916	13/09/1916
War Diary	Buire	14/09/1916	17/09/1916
War Diary	Fricourt	18/09/1916	30/09/1916
Heading	21st Div. 38th Sanitary Section Oct 1916		
War Diary	Fricourt	01/10/1916	01/10/1916
War Diary	Buire	02/10/1916	03/10/1916
War Diary	Ailly-Le-Haut-Clocher	04/10/1916	08/10/1916
War Diary	Noeux-Les-Mines	09/10/1916	10/10/1916
War Diary	Sailly-Labourse	11/10/1916	31/10/1916
Heading	21st Div 38th Sanitary Section Nov 1916		
War Diary	Sailly Labourse	01/11/1916	30/11/1916
Heading	21st Div 38th Sanitary Section Dec 1916		
War Diary	Sailly-Labourse	01/12/1916	27/12/1916
War Diary	Labeuvriere	28/12/1916	31/12/1916
Heading	21st Div 38th Sanitary Section Jan 1917		
War Diary	Labeuvriere	01/01/1917	28/01/1917
War Diary	Wormhoudt	29/01/1917	31/01/1917
Heading	21st Div 38th Sanitary Section Feb 1917		
War Diary	Wormhoudt	01/02/1917	11/02/1917
War Diary	Bethune	12/02/1917	14/02/1917
War Diary	Sailly-Labourse	15/02/1917	28/02/1917
Heading	21st Div No. 38 Sanitary Section Mar 1917		
War Diary	Sailly-Labourse	01/03/1917	11/03/1917
War Diary	Lucheux	12/03/1917	28/03/1917
War Diary	Bavincourt	29/03/1917	31/03/1917

WO 95
2148/3

38 Sanitary Section

30TH SANITARY SECTION

SEP 1915 – SEP 1916
1917 MAR

21ST DIVISION

To 3 ARMY

21st Division

Summarised but not copied

121/7121

S.

Sept '15

21st Divisional Sanitary Sect. (No 38)

Vol I

Sept 15

Dec '16

WAR DIARY or INTELLIGENCE SUMMARY

Army Form C.2118

Place	Date	Hour	Summary of Events and Information	Remarks and references to Appendices
Milford	11/9/15	12.15 pm	Entrained Milford Station for Southampton Docks	
"	"	2.25 pm	Arrived Southampton Docks	
"	"	5.30 pm	Embarked per S/S Chybassa	
Havre	12/9/15	10.30 am	Disembarked	
"	"	2 pm	Entrained	
Audruicque	13/9/15	11 am	Detrained	
"	"	12 noon	Marched to Watten to join 21st Divisional Headquarters	
Watten	"	4 pm	~~Arrived~~ Reported arrival to Div. Hd. Qrs.	
	13/9/15 to 20/9/15		Billeted at Watten. Sanitary Arrangements at Watten were considerably improved by the Section. Water tested and found fairly good. Pipe Supply to Dunkirk is obtainable at certain times & places only. Drainage at Div. Hd Qrs bad & improved. Incinerators was erected for use of Div Hd Qrs. Had several carcases improperly buried by the French treated with Chloride of Lime.	
	20/9/15	5 pm	Left Watten	
	20-21 Sept 1915 midnight	midnight	Arrived at Racquinghem spent up at Chateau de Sorbonne	
	21/9/15	8 pm	Water supply here very bad requiring maximum chlorine treatment. Left Racquinghem	
	21-22 Sept 1915	12 mid	Arrived St Hilaire	
	22/9/15	6 pm	Left St Hilaire	
		9 pm	Arrived Ferfay Chateau. Water good	

Army Form C. 2118

WAR DIARY
or
~~INTELLIGENCE SUMMARY~~

(Erase heading not required.)

Place	Date	Hour	Summary of Events and Information	Remarks and references to Appendices
~~Mazingarbe~~	23/9/15	3 am	Bivouacked	
Mazingarbe	24/9/15	9 am	Left for Mazingarbe	
Nœux les Mines	"	12.30 pm	Arrived Mazingarbe but found place being shelled so moved on to La Philosophe	
La Philosophe	24/9/15	2 pm	Arrived here. took up quarters. Stayed here until the 29th. Place under shell fire during this time. This is a very unsanitary area. Water has generally good being from chalk wells. Buried 2 mules & 3 horses during this time. This place is in ruins. The Division took part in the engagement for Loos.	
	29/9/15		Left for Bethune	
	30/9/15		Arrived at Leuttie Chateau — A bad billeting area. Accommodation for troops bad & limited. The Chateau is dilapidated.	

A. Schofield
Lieut R.A.M.C.T
O.C Sanitary Section
21st Division

21st Division

Summarised but not copied

Oct 1915

21/7595

38th Sanitary Section
21st Div:

Vol 2

Oct 15

WAR DIARY or INTELLIGENCE SUMMARY

Army Form C. 2118

(Erase heading not required.)

Place	Date	Hour	Summary of Events and Information	Remarks and references to Appendices
Morbecque	1/10/15	2 pm	Arrived at Morbecque from Lillers. Put up at billets for the night. Billeting accommodation fair	
Hondeghem	2/10/15	5 pm	Arrived here from Morbecque — Accommodation good, village comparatively clean and water generally good. Fine modern church here. Stayed here in billets for 4 days. Roads in this neighbourhood in very fair order. Some foot & mouth disease at several farms in the neighbourhood	
Merris	6/10/15	1 pm	Arrived here from Hondeghem & went into Billets — Accommodation not so good as at Hondeghem & village not clean or so well kept. A poorer neighbourhood. L'Hospice here is a large building very suitable for a hospital if necessary or for a Divisional Head Quarters for which purpose it is being used. L'Hospice was shelled by the Germans when they were here & the church has been considerably damaged also by the Germans inside. The water here is generally good. Some wells are bad however including the public well in the main street. Water at Caestre Brewery was found to be good spring	
"	7/10/15		Generally speaking the water in this neighbourhood is unreliable only the deep well at Brewery Caestre can be counted upon as being pure. Most of the water is from shallow wells. There is a good spring at Outtersteene — water is scarce at Pradelles & Borre. The soil is a heavy clay. There are two good bathing ponds near Merris south of the Hazebrouck-Armentières line	
	8/10/15		nil	
	9/10/15		nil	
	10/10/15		nil	

WAR DIARY or INTELLIGENCE SUMMARY

Army Form C. 2118

Place	Date	Hour	Summary of Events and Information	Remarks and references to Appendices
Merris	11/10/15		Nil	
"	12/10/15		Nil	
	13/10/15		Nil	
	14/10/15		Nil	
	15/10/15		Nil	
	16/10/15		Nil	
	17/10/15		Nil	
	18/10/15		Nil	
	19/10/15		Nil	
	20/10/15		It having been decided to make the Merris District a permanent Divisional billeting area, complete water tests have been made at the following places: Merris, Strazeele, Pradelles, Borre, Caestre, Outtersteene, & all the principle wells & billets and permanent notices fixed to pumps & wells showing results of tests. Also permanent incinerators are being erected at all important places.	
	21/10/15		Nil	
	22/10/15		Nil	
	23/10/15		Nil	
	24/10/15		Nil	
	25/10/15		Nil	
	26/10/15		Nil	
	27/10/15		Nil	
	28/10/15		Nil	
	29/10/15		Nil	
	30/10/15		Nil	
	31/10/15		The weather has set in very wet with the result that the roads, most of which are improperly macadamised, are getting badly cut up.	

R.J. Schofield
Lieut RAMC
O.C. Sanitary Section 38
2nd Division

S

Dec 1915

21st Div

Summarised but not copied Vol: 4

38th Sany Section

San: Sect: No: 38

Vol: 4

121/7931

Confidential

War Diary

of

O/c. N°38 Sanitary Section - 21st Division.

from 1st Dec 1915 to 31st Dec 1915

WAR DIARY or INTELLIGENCE SUMMARY

Army Form C. 2118

(Erase heading not required.)

Place	Date 1915	Hour	Summary of Events and Information	Remarks and references to Appendices
Field	1st Oct		Visited Pont de Nieppe Baths and found them satisfactory. Lieut Eades 95th Field Ambulance arrived for duty today to carry out inspection with a view to the early diagnosis of Scabies.	
	2nd		Visited the baths at Asylum and billets in that area. The Bathing accommodation for officers is being taken advantage of to a considerable degree.	
	3rd		Visited the Refuse Dumps at PRES DUHEM and BLUE BLIND FACTORY. These cope with most of the refuse of the town of ARMENTIERES both civil and military.	
	4		The street cleansing which used to be done by civilian labour is not satisfactory and parties from the Composite Co will do the work till other arrangements are made.	
	5		I visited Pont de Nieppe Baths and found that the work there continues satisfactory. Several cases of Scabies have been discovered and dealt with.	
	6		The Baths do not work on Sundays and in consequence the boilers are overhauled and on Mondays there is a much better supply of steam and water. This was very noticeable today.	
	7		The Refuse Dump at PRES.DUHEM is very unsatisfactory today owing to the flooding. The approach road is very muddy and if the river rises it may be necessary to close it down.	
	8		To-day I visited the principal streets and found the work of cleansing carried out by the Composite Co under a Sanitary N.C.O. has improved matters a bit. but if the proper cleansing plant could be brought into use it would be more satisfactory.	
	9		To day I went round with the Civil Vidangeur and superintended the emptying of cesspools in several billets. The sanitary corporal goes round as a rule with him and points out the cesspools to empty and sees the work carried out. During bombardment of the town this afternoon. No.2611 Act Sgt Icker was wounded by shrapnel and sent to hospital. A shell struck the Hdqr billet of the section and did damage to equipment. A shell also struck the O.C.s billet.	
	10th		No 2625 Pte Jones reported for duty from Base to-day. Asylum Baths visited and found satisfactory.	

WAR DIARY or ~~INTELLIGENCE SUMMARY~~

(Erase heading not required.)

Army Form C. 2118

Instructions regarding War Diaries and Intelligence Summaries are contained in F. S. Regs., Part II. and the Staff Manual respectively. Title Pages will be prepared in manuscript.

Place	Date 1915	Hour	Summary of Events and Information	Remarks and references to Appendices
Field	Dec 11th	—	Visited Bailleul and inspected Refuse Dump there and also Sanitary Exhibition. Total number bathed at Pont de Nieppe Baths for week 6495.	
	12	—	Visited Refuse Dumps at Asile des Alienes and Blue Blind and found these able to cope with all Refuse	
	13	—	Baths at Pont de Nieppe were unable to work to-day on account of flooding	
	14		Baths working to-day under difficulty — over two feet of water in engine room. Lieut Schurr of 63rd Field Ambulance appointed to take charge of RAMC details at Baths to-day.	
	15		Water in Baths going down rapidly	
	16		Visited several billets throughout the Town. Sample meat safes have been made from materials at hand such as packing cases and biscuit tins. These will be on view at Divisional Sanitary Office and officers are invited to inspect them	
	17		Inspected Divisional Baths at Pont de Nieppe and Asile des Alienes and found work satisfactory	
	18		Inspected water pumps and stand pipes at Pont de Nieppe and carried out water tests by Horrocks method. No. Bathed at Pont de Nieppe during week - 6586	
	19		Case of Scarlet Fever was notified in Rue D'Erquinghem. Armentières. I visited the patient and gave the necessary directions for isolation.	
	20		A box has been made for the hose pipe at N. end of Rue d'Erquinghem to prevent it being left on the ground	
	21		A dead horse belonging to a civilian in Armentières had to transported to the horse Cemetery at Sheet 38 H 6. b.d. and burnt by this unit	
	22		Inspected the Divisional Baths at Pont de Nieppe and Asile des Alienes	
	23		A case of Diphtheria in a civilian child was notified in Rue de la Lys Pont de Nieppe. I visited the house and gave the necessary directions for isolation and placed the house out of bounds	
	24		Visited the principal streets and found these had been kept clean. There are now 6 instead of 4 GS waggons at our disposal for collecting street refuse.	

WAR DIARY or INTELLIGENCE SUMMARY

Place	Date 1915	Hour	Summary of Events and Information	Remarks and references to Appendices
Field	Dec 25th	—	Divisional Baths closed to-day. No bathers for week at Pont de Nieppe 4871.	
	26th		Case of Scarlet Fever reported at 31 Rue St Honoré. I visited the house and found that the patient, a young girl, had been removed to Hospital at Rue Sadi Carnot.	
	27th		Divisional Baths had to be closed owing to engine defect. Foden Disinfecting Lorry was used to day by this division.	
	28th		Two cases of measles reported to me to day. One in an officer of 1st Lincolns and the other in a Pte of 64th Field Ambulance. Precautions were taken to prevent spread of infection. There was no evidence to show that the two cases were associated in any way. An officer of the 1st Lincolns who occupies the same billet as the sick officer was also sent away for isolation as he presented some suspicious symptoms.	
	29th		Pte Dearman No 201 reported to day for duty to replace casualty.	
	30th		The Baths programme for next week was made up from returns sent in as called for in ARO 364	
	31st		I visited the Refuse Dump to day. Attention was drawn to the large amount of serviceable material collected in the Refuse Dump and returns to salvage by this unit.	

21st D.

Jan 1916

F/259/1

38th San. Sect.
vol: 5
Jan '16

Confidential

War Diary of No 38 Sanitary Section
from 1st to 31st January 1916.

AMiddleton Shore
H Rawes

O.C. SANITARY SECTION
21st DIVISION.

WAR DIARY or INTELLIGENCE SUMMARY

Army Form C. 2118

(Erase heading not required.)

Place	Date 1916	Hour	Summary of Events and Information	Remarks and references to Appendices
Armentieres	1 January		Total number bathed during week ending today (five days) at Divisional Baths - 6972	
	2nd		nil	
	3rd		A Foden Lorry disinfector has arrived at Pont de Nieppe. This will be used by this Division 3 days a week.	
	4th		A case of Scarlet Fever occurred in the 12th N.F's. An outbreak of Tonsillitis was investigated in 14th N.F's	
	5th		Refuse Dump at Asile des Aliénés abandoned today owing to shellfire.	
	6th		Visited 25th Divisional Baths at Pont de Nieppe	
	7th		Various sources of water at Houplines were visited and tested today by Horrocks Method. Sheet cleaning plant belonging to M. Prevot which it is proposed to take over was inspected.	
	8th		A case of Scarlet Fever was notified today in Bois Fairheribe. This was visited and the house put out of bounds. — 8391 men bathed at Divisional Baths during week ending today.	
	9th		In absence of O/c Composite Co. I held an inspection of that Co. today	
	10th		nil	
	11th		Visited sources of water at Pont de Nieppe and carried out tests. All those in use were found satisfactory	
	12th		Inspected town water works in Rue Mesures. The supply is 68 cub. metres per hour from a deep well. It is pumped into a Tower and supplies the town by gravitation.	
	13th		nil	
	14th		nil	
	15th		Bath at Pont de Nieppe had to be closed for repairs. One case of Measles notified in 64th Field Ambulance 7495 men were bathed at Divisional Baths during week ending today. (5 days)	
	16th		nil	
	17th		Two samples of water from a source near Hanches were submitted for analysis. Poisonous Metals, Arsenic, Antimony and Cyanides were found absent. The billet at Rue hamantine occupied by the Sanitary Section was shelled this evening. Cpl Howarth and Sgt Dewhurst were wounded and some equipment was damaged.	
	18th		Sanitary Section moved into New Billet at ECOLE PROFESSIONALE.	
	19th		Four portable Horsfal Disinfectors have been delivered for use at Central Refuse Dump.	
	20th		nil	
	21st		nil	
	22nd		8258 men were bathed at Divisional Baths during week ending today.	
	23rd		nil	
	24th		Street sweeping vehicles have been removed to R.E. Park for repair and overhauling.	
	25th		nil	
	26th		12 brushes, 6 mud scrapers, 6 shovels and 3 scoops and 1 brush for Rotary mud sweeper were taken over for street cleaning from Prevot.	

WAR DIARY or INTELLIGENCE SUMMARY

Army Form C. 2118

Place	Date 1916	Hour	Summary of Events and Information	Remarks and references to Appendices
Armentieres	Jany 27th		nil	
	28th		nil	
	29th		9316 men were bathed at Diversion Baths during week ending to-day. Central water-supply cut off to-day owing to shell fire injuring plant	
	30th		Visited the various units in the area to arrange about temporary supply of water from local wells	
	31st		nil	

No. 38 Sanitary Section.

Feb. 1916.

San: Sect 38
Vol: 6

— Confidential —

War Diary
of
N° 38 Sanitary Section
from 1st February till 29th Feby 1916

WAR DIARY or INTELLIGENCE SUMMARY

(Erase heading not required.)

Army Form C. 2118

38th SANITARY SECTION
21st DIVISION

Place	Date	Hour	Summary of Events and Information	Remarks and references to Appendices
ARMENTIERES	February 1916 1	—	A table was made up showing the difference between the numbers applied for for bathing weekly and numbers reporting at Divisional Baths. This has been sent out to the Infantry & Artillery Brigades	
	2	—	One mud tank for collecting street mud was taken into use	
	3	—	Motor Lorry was returned from DSC after repairs	
	4	—	The O.C. F.A.W. has taken over the mechanical supervision of the Foden Lorry Disinfector	
	5	—	7873 men bathed at Divisional Baths during week ending to-day.	
	6	—	A programme for collecting refuse of civilians from various streets daily in rotation has been drawn up to day	
	7	—	nil	
	8	—	A suspected case of Scarlet Fever occurred to day in a man who returned from leave three days ago. The necessary disinfection and other precautionary measures have been carried out. Additional washing is being carried out at Headquarters laundry to-day to assist the laundry at Divisional Baths.	
	9	—	A rotary mud sweeping brush has now been taken into use in the area	
	10	—	nil	
	11	—	Shortly after noon to-day a shell struck the Divisional Baths and exploded in the Boiling Room. There were no casualties but a good deal of damage was done to machinery and clothing.	
	12	—	Bathing at Divisional Baths is still being carried on; and a certain amount of washing. 8068 men were bathed during week ending to-day	
	13	—	A rotary mud brush has been requisitioned from Hornshin for use in the area.	
	14	—	A bomb and shell proof shelter is to be built for the civilians employed at the Divisional Baths. The work was commenced to-day	
	15	—	nil	
	16	—	nil	
	17	—	Billeting certificates for Divisional Baths from 9th Nov 15 - 31st Jany 16 were filled up and sent off to day	
	18	—	A complaint that "lousy" clothing was being issued from the Divisional Baths to the 10th KOYLI Regiment was investigated and found to be without foundation	
	19	—	7809 men bathed at Divisional Baths during week ending to-day	
	20	—	nil	
	21	—	Representations have been made with a view to having less serviceable material sent to the Refuse Dump along with the Billet Refuse. A good deal of time has to be spent daily searching the material and collecting for salvage	

WAR DIARY or INTELLIGENCE SUMMARY

Army Form C. 2118

Place	Date	Hour	Summary of Events and Information	Remarks and references to Appendices
	February 1916			
ARMENTIERES	22	—	Permission was granted to erect a urinal for use of troops at Pont de Nieppe on the vacant ground at corner of Route Nationale and Rue Rivage	
	23	—	Capt Thevaus RAMC T has taken over charge of details at Divisional Bath in place of Capt Schwn Rawc	
	24	—	nil	
	25	—	To day I visited the sanitary arrangements of the 25th Division at Merris etc	
	26	—	A suspected case of Measles in an officer of the 10th Yorks regiment reported and necessary action taken to prevent spread. 7448 men bathed at Divisional Bath during week ending to-day	
	27	—	nil	
	28	—	A specially wired incinerator has been built at the Refuse Dump to deal with wet stable refuse	
	29	—	Monthly medical board of Composite Co. att Sanitary Section was held to day	

March 1916

Confidential

War Diary
of
No 38 Sanitary Section

from 1st March 1916 till 31st March 1916.

Middleton Davies
O.C. SANITARY SECTION
21st DIVISION.

38 San Sec
Vol 7

WAR DIARY or INTELLIGENCE SUMMARY

Army Form C. 2118

Place	Date March 1916	Hour	Summary of Events and Information	Remarks and references to Appendices
ARMENTIERES	1st		The approach to the dump is very soft following the recent rains. The roadway is being improved slightly by laying down ashes from the Divisional Baths.	
	2nd		A suspected case of Measles in an officer of the 10th Y.L. was reported today. The billet occupied by him has meantime been put out of bounds.	
	3rd		Nil	
	4th		A verminous officers billet was inspected today in Bde Faidherbe; steps were taken to rid it of the vermin. 8087 men were bathed at divisional baths for week ending today.	
	5th		I saw M Grimonpont to-day along with the DAA & QMG. It was resolved to pay 5 frs per metre removed for cleaning of cesspits in the area.	
	6th		A suspected case of infectious disease reported by O/c 63rd Field Ambulance in 38 Rue de Messines was visited to-day. No action was taken. The suspected case of measles of 2/III/16 has not been confirmed; one case of measles in officer of Somerset Light Infantry occurred to-day. Disinfection of billet etc was carried out.	
	7th		Visited Pont de Nieppe Area. An accumulation of Horse Manure behind the Field Ambulance was brought to the notice of the O/C.	
	8th		Nil	
	9th		2nd Lieut Day 9th K.O.Y.L.I. reported to take command of Composite Co. attached Sanitary Section N° 38	
	10th		A case of CSF has occurred in the SW Borderers. This unit left this area on 5th inst. Their billet has been disinfected before being occupied by other troops.	
	11th		Total number bathed at Divisional Baths during week ending to-day 8917	
	12th		Case of Measles notified in 64th Bde Machine Gunners. This unit is at present in the trenches. arrangements have been made to disinfect the billet last occupied by them.	
	13th		Went over the area with O/c Sanitary Section 17th Division.	
	14th		Visited MERRIS area with O/c Sanitary Section 17th Division.	
	15th		One case of Measles, and one case of Scarlet Fever have been notified to-day. The necessary disinfection has been carried out.	
	16th		1880 francs received to-day in payment for sanitary administration of civil population from 25th Jany till 11th March. as per contract.	
	17th		Nil	
	18th		One case of Measles notified in 8th Somersets. The necessary disinfection has been carried out. Total number bathed this week at Divisional Baths 9669.	

WAR DIARY or INTELLIGENCE SUMMARY

Army Form C. 2118

(Erase heading not required.)

Place	Date	Hour	Summary of Events and Information	Remarks and references to Appendices
	March 1916			
ARMENTIERES	19th		One case of Measles notified in 63rd Trench Mortar Battery. The necessary disinfection has been carried out	
"	20th		Visited billets evacuated by 63rd Bde & found these satisfactory	
"	21		nil	
"	22		Marched out of ARMENTIERES and took over billets in MERRIS area.	
MERRIS	23		Inspected bathing facilities in the new area and made necessary arrangements to commence the bathing of troops.	
	24		Visited 5 German Measles contacts left in this area by 17th Division.	
	25		Went to PONT de NIEPPE baths to pay finally the civilian employees there	
	26		nil	
	27		One case of Measles notified in a driver of 64th FA. at LA CRECHE. Disinfection carried out.	
	28		nil	
	29		nil	
	30		One case of Scarlet Fever — subsequently diagnosed as German Measles — notified in 97 Bde RFA at LA BREARDE. Visited the billet & took necessary precautions	
	31		Paid off civilian employees of Divisional Baths at METEREN, Steenwerck and OOTERSTEENE	

O.C. SANITARY SECTION
21st DIVISION.

April 1916

WAR DIARY

38th *Sanitary Section*
21st Divisional Sanitary Section

for

April 1916

WAR DIARY or INTELLIGENCE SUMMARY

(Erase heading not required.)

Army Form C. 2118

21 Div San Sec
No 38 S.S.
Vol

Place	Date	Hour	Summary of Events and Information	Remarks and references to Appendices
	April 1916			
MERRIS	1		The section marched out of Merris at 1 p.m. to entraining station.	
RIBEMONT	2		Arrived at Longpry at 6.30 a.m. by rail. Thence to Ribemont by motor charabanc which was reached by 10.30 a.m. Inspected billets of men.	
	3		Went over the forward part of the area with O/C San Sect 7th Division and visited bath houses at Ville and Méaulte.	
	4		Sanitation in Ribemont very defective. Will require to be reorganised.	
	5		Visited divisional bath house at Le Neuville and arranged to commence working it.	
	6		A site has been chosen for central incinerators at Ribemont and two incinerators have been built.	
	7		Two squads of men each under an acting sgt have been sent to the outlying parts of the area.	
	8		Refuse dumps at Buire, Ville, and Méaulte have been chosen.	
	9		Nil	
	10		Inspected well at Headquarters R.E. billet. Advised 2 scoopfuls bleaching powder per 10 gallons.	
	11		Visited support trenches of Divisional Area.	
	12		Sent nose and throat swabs from suspected Diphtheria carrier at Méaulte to No 10 Mob Laboratory.	
	13		Pte Neal reported from base for duty with section.	
	14		Visited disinfecting station at Morlancourt. Made arrangements for divisional disinfecting.	
	15		Billet No 11 Méaulte has been placed out of bounds as a civilian diphtheria carrier stays there.	
	16		A case of C.S. Fever notified in 178th Tunnelling Co at Méaulte. The contacts have been isolated and the O/C No 10 Mob Laboratory informed and asked to investigate them.	
	17		Sites for public latrines have been chosen at Buire.	
	18		Visited sanitary arrangements at Le Neuville with A.D.M.S.	
	19		One GS waggon at Buire and one at Ville has been placed at disposal of Town Major for sanitary cartage.	
	20		Pte Pike M.E. reported for duty from base.	

WAR DIARY or INTELLIGENCE SUMMARY

Army Form C. 2118

(Erase heading not required.)

Place	Date	Hour	Summary of Events and Information	Remarks and references to Appendices
RIBEMONT	21/4/16		Capt: A.M. Brown R.A.M.C. Contracted German Measles. Duty taken over by CAPT. J.S.C. HOLDEN R.A.M.C. 6y/th Field Ambulance. Arrangements made with A.D.V.S. re disposal of dead horses. Site of burial places fixed.	[initials]
"	22/4/16		Inspected Divisional Baths at LA NEUVILLE. Supply of clean clothing unsatisfactory - arranged for weekly statement to be supplied showing stock issued & stock in hand. - Visited Baths at VILLE MILL	[initials]
"	23/4/16		Visited billets in VILLE occupied by Officers of 63rd Bde M.G. Coy. from which Lieut. DES VOEUX had been removed suffering from Cerebrospinal [meningitis] (Diagnosis confirmed by wire from Highland C.C.S.). As his Coy. were just moving back to BONNAY - arranged for isolation of all Officers - Sgt Major - Officers Cooks & servants in BONNAY & for bacteriological examination to be made by O/c No 10 Mobile Lab. Inspected Sanitary arrangements in hand at BUIRE & VILLE	[initials]
"	24/4/16		Paid visits to MÉAULTE & BONNAY to inspect sanitary arrangements. Found very little attempt in either place to keep billets clean or dispose of proper manure.	[initials]
"	25/4/16		Found suitable buildings at RIBEMONT MILL to establish small bathing establishment for men attached to H.Q. - applied for necessary materials to carry on alteration	[initials]
"	26/4/16		By arrangements had 6th M.O. permits stationed at BUSSY LES DAOURS, DAOURS & VECQUEMONT to arrange suitable sites for incinerators & public latrines & urinals. Inspected billets & horse lines. Interviewed Town Major & promised him help from Sanitary Section	[initials]
"	27/4/16		Interviewed Town Major - BUIRE & arranged sites for central incinerators & also for latrines to urinals	[initials]

WAR DIARY
or
INTELLIGENCE SUMMARY
(Erase heading not required.)

Army Form C. 2118

Instructions regarding War Diaries and Intelligence Summaries are contained in F. S. Regs., Part II. and the Staff Manual respectively. Title Pages will be prepared in manuscript.

Place	Date	Hour	Summary of Events and Information	Remarks and references to Appendices
RIBEMONT	28/4/16		Visited baths at LANEUVILLE - work impeded owing to lack of clean clothing. The laundry at CERISY which has undertaken to wash clothing from div. baths cannot return clean clothing under 10 days from time of receipt. Saw No. 10 Mobile Laboratory re C.S.M. contacts	[initials]
"	29/4/16		Inspected work in progress at RIBEMONT MILL constructing div. baths - collected 9 baths for use there from Salvage Corps.	[initials]
"	30/4/16		Visited VILLE refuse dump & found incinerators insufficient to cope with amount of refuse - arrangements made for construction of 2 extra.	

Sandys J. C. Holden
Capt. R.A.M.C.
Acting O/c 21st Division
Sanitary Section

May 1916

38 San Sec
Vol 9

— Confidential —

War Diary for May 1916.

Williston Lynn
Capt of

COMMITTEE FOR THE
MEDICAL HISTORY OF THE WAR

Date 26 JUN 1919

WAR DIARY or INTELLIGENCE SUMMARY

Army Form C. 2118

(Erase heading not required.)

Place	1916 Date May	Hour	Summary of Events and Information	Remarks and references to Appendices
Field	1		nil	
	2		Reported outbreak of C.S.M. in 63rd Bde. M.G. Coy. investigated	
	3		Inspected sanitation of billets occupied by French Troops in RIBEMONT.	
	4		nil	
	5		Visited Queens Redoubt and Right Section and reported to A.D.M.S. on sanitation there. Ville Mill laundry taken over from 18th Div.	
	6		Two sets of bathing apparatus arrived - one set fitted up at Ribemont Mill as bath house for Headquarters troops.	
	7		Bath House at RIBEMONT opened for use	
	8		Visited Laundry at Cagny and Bureau de Bienfaisance at AMIENS with reference to washing and repair of clothing from Divisional Baths.	
	9		Visited DAOURS and LA NEUVILLE to inspect sanitary progress.	
	10		Breakdown at Ville Mill Baths - part of flooring collapsed	
	11		Visited Queens Redoubt - can report no progress in sanitation. Found bath-house at MEAULTE had been broken into and occupied by an Artillery Bde. of 34th Div.	
	12		Went over La Neuville with Town Major	
	13		Visited BUIRE and Ville and inspected sanitation.	
	14		O.C. reported off leave following attack of German Measles.	
	15		Proceeded to Cagny and paid 1241·17 frs. for washing.	
	16		Visited lines of Corps H.A. west of RIBEMONT and advised re sanitation.	
	17		The boiler of the bathing apparatus at RIBEMONT MILL leaks and has been sent to O/C Div Supply Col. for repair	
	18		Visited Queen Redoubt - very little progress yet to report.	
	19		Visited BUIRE and VILLE and inspected sanitation there.	
	20		Re-visited Queens Redoubt - sanitation slightly improved	
	21		Inspected sanitation in RIBEMONT and adjacent part of area towards HEILLY	
	22		Visited lines of 91st Bde R.F.A. along with O.C. & M.O. and inspected sanitation. Additional incinerators required to deal with manure	

WAR DIARY
~~INTELLIGENCE SUMMARY~~
(Erase heading not required.)

Army Form C. 2118

Place	Date May 1916	Hour	Summary of Events and Information	Remarks and references to Appendices
RIBEMONT	23	—	Visited 94th Bde Horse lines - The latrines in three batteries are defective - reported to M.O. (in action)	
	24	—	Proceeded to CAGNY to pay laundry bill and then to AMIENS to arrange mending of clothing.	
	25	—	Visited billets evacuated by French troops yesterday - these were left very dirty.	
	26	—	Visited billets in Ribemont and MEAULTE.	
	27	—	Inspected La Neuville baths - The apparatus for heating water is out of action	
	28	—	Bath apparatus at La Neuville taken down for inspection - pump requires adjusting and has been sent to Divisional Workshops.	
	29	—	Case of Scarlet Fever in civilian in La Neuville - visited and had billets in farm evacuated and put out of bounds. There is no accommodation for this patient in the local hospital and the case must be nursed at home.	
	30	—	nil	
	31	—	Proceeded to AMIENS and paid 91frs for repair of socks at Bureau de Bienfaisance. Took sample of white wine from estaminet at MEAULTE to No 12 Mobile Laboratory for analysis.	

38 San Sec.
Vol 10
June

June 1916

Confidential

War Diary of
No 38 Sanitary Section
for June 1916

COMMITTEE FOR THE
MEDICAL HISTORY OF THE WAR
Date 5 AUG. 1916

WAR DIARY or INTELLIGENCE SUMMARY

(Erase heading not required.)

Army Form C. 2118

Instructions regarding War Diaries and Intelligence Summaries are contained in F. S. Regs., Part II. and the Staff Manual respectively. Title Pages will be prepared in manuscript.

38th SANITARY SECTION / 21st DIVISION

Place	Date June 1916	Hour	Summary of Events and Information	Remarks and references to Appendices
RIBEMONT.	1st		Made a tour of inspection of estaminets frequented by Troops and gave necessary instructions re sanitation	
	2nd		Pte Ruth reported from base as reinforcement. The section is now up to full strength.	
	3rd		Visited Cheshire Labour Batt" in camp near Meaulte and gave sanitary instructions to O.C.	
	4th		Visited LA NEUVILLE area	
	5th		Visited estaminets and cafés in BOIRE to see if these were kept sanitary while frequented by Troops. One or two require to be cleaned and on threatening to advise that they be put "out of bounds" to troops, the owners promised to take the necessary action.	
	6th		Made a tour of inspection of water supplies of RIBEMONT.	
	7th		Visited Queens Redoubt and inspected sanitation there. Three box fly proof latrines for deep trench have been made by this section and supplied for use in this area.	
	8th		nil	
	9th		Visited MEAULTE and found the Bath house there occupied by D Batty 182nd Bde RFA. A letter has been written forwarded asking if they have authority to use it.	
	10th		Visited billet occupied by 149 Corp Co RE and submitted report to A.D.M.S.	
	11th		Visited camp of 7th Volunteer of 17th Div between BOIRE and VILLE and gave sanitary instructions to M.O i/c.	
	12th		nil	
	13th		Suspected case of Diphtheria in man of 185 Co ASC.	
	14th		Visited camp of 185 Co ASC and had all contacts of suspected Diphtheria case paraded and examined. Took throat and nose brushings of close contacts	
	15th		Visited site of proposed Adv Field Amb. and arranged sites for latrines and urinal.	
	16th		Proceeded to Cogney and Amiens to pay accounts for washing and repair of clothing.	
	17th		nil	
	18th		Supervised burial of six horses killed by shell fire at Meaulte yesterday.	
	19th		The washing machine at Ville Mill has broken down: and washing is meantime suspended.	
	20th		nil	
	21st		Pte Neal (attached) suffers from shell shock. He has been transferred to LA NEUVILLE chalet for duty	

WAR DIARY or INTELLIGENCE SUMMARY

Army Form C. 2118

(Erase heading not required.)

Instructions regarding War Diaries and Intelligence Summaries are contained in F. S. Regs., Part II. and the Staff Manual respectively. Title Pages will be prepared in manuscript.

38th SANITARY SECTION
21st DIVISION

Place	Date June 1916	Hour	Summary of Events and Information	Remarks and references to Appendices
RIBEMONT	22nd		Visited sanitations in BUIRE and VILLE districts along with N CO i/c.	
	23rd		The washing machine at VILLE MILL is again in working order.	
	24th		nil	
	25th		Visited MERICOURT and site of 64th Field Amb. A refuse dump near the Ambulance requires immediate attention.	
	26th		The refuse dump near ambulance at MERICOURT is being cleaned up by a fatigue party from 63rd Fd Ambulance	
	27th		Visited Caqny and Amiens to pay accounts for washing and repair of clothing.	
	28th		nil	
	29th		Baths at La NEUVILLE given up and billeting certificate submitted.	
	30th		nil	

Capt. R.A.M.C.
O.C. SANITARY SECTION
21st DIVISION.

July 1916

21st Div'n

38th Sanity Section

July. 1916

COMMITTEE FOR THE
MEDICAL HISTORY OF THE WAR

Date   5 - SEP. 1916

WAR DIARY or **INTELLIGENCE SUMMARY**

Army Form C.2118

MEDICAL July
21

38th SANITARY SECTION — 21st DIVISION — Vol IV

Place	Date July	Hour	Summary of Events and Information	Remarks and references to Appendices
RIBEMONT	1	—	Division attacking. Routine duties by Section. O.C. on duty at 64th Field Ambulance	
	2	—	Ville Mill laundry and baths are being run by Section. O.C. on duty at 64th Fd Amb.	
	3	—	Party sent up under O.C. to attempt to improve sanitation in Queens Redoubt which had been neglected during operations of last two days.	
	4	—	Section moved to Belloy-sur-Somme. Baths etc handed over to 17th Divn.	
BELLOY sur Somme	5	—	Additional stores transferred from Ribemont. Routine duties at Belloy-sur-Somme. Sanitary arrangements in village practically nil.	
	6	—	Arranged baths at Picquigny and Ailly-sur-Somme.	
	7	—	Section moved to Cavillon. Sanitation of village very bad	
Cavillon	8	—	Routine duties. O.C. visited Brigade areas. Clean clothing from Cagny laundry issued to Brigades	
	9	—	Routine duties	
	10	—	Section moved to Ville-sur-Ancre. Baths and laundry taken over from 17th Divn	
Ville sur Ancre	11	—	Party attached to burying party in rear of fighting. Inspected Fricourt and neighbourhood and found no unburied dead	
	12	—	Routine duties. Re-organised Ville Mill Baths & Laundry. Sanitary duties in Ville which was found very dirty and neglected.	
	13	—	Routine duties	
	14 15 16 17	—	O.C. and 20 O.R. on duty at 64th Field Amb. Remainder working Baths at Ville	
	18	—	Routine duties. Visited German cemetery at Fricourt which had been shelled on 17th and when several bodies were exposed. The nuisance complained of by the 21 Divn R.F.A. was abated	

WAR DIARY or INTELLIGENCE SUMMARY

Army Form C. 2118

(Erase heading not required.)

Place	Date	Hour	Summary of Events and Information
Ville sur Ancre	19	—	Bathed and issued clean clothing to 110th Bde at Ribemont and to 62nd Bde at Ville.
	20	—	Section moved to Cavillon.
Cavillon	21	—	Returned to Ville and acting on orders from D.O.M.S 15th Corps I handed over Baths Laundry fittings and stock to 51st Divn. A quantity of clean clothing was removed from Cagny Laundry and handed over to 15th Corps Laundry at Heilly.
	22	—	Train party under Sgt. Sutcliffe proceeded by lorry to entrain at Longeau.
	23	—	Section moved to Le Cauroy.
Le Cauroy	24	—	Routine duties. — Baths at Berlincourt taken over and now working.
	25	—	Routine duties
	26	—	Visited Duisans and Halvus and saw DADMS 14th Divn.
	27	—	Routine duties. details of 64th Bde bathed at Berlincourt. visited laundry and Baths at Louez along with DADMS.
	28	—	Advance parties sent to villages in new area. Hautville. Wanquetin. Agnez. and Duisans.
	29	—	Routine duties - baths arranged for 10th KOYLI at Wanquetin
	30	—	Section moved to Duisans.
Duisans	31	—	Routine duties.

McMahon
Capt RAMC

21st Div.

Aug. 1916

38th San. Sect.

WAR
CONFIDENTIAL
DIARY
for
AUGUST 1916

Vol 12

A.Middleton Shaw
O.C. SANITARY SECTION
21st DIVISION.

WAR DIARY or INTELLIGENCE SUMMARY

MEDICAL
Army Form C. 2118

Place	Date	Hour	Summary of Events and Information	Remarks and references to Appendices
DUISANS –	1916 August 1st		Inspected a Platoon of 13th N.F's along with their M.O at St Nicholas – These were contacts of a Scarlet Fever Case. No sign of this was found amongst these contacts	
	2		Cpl Dutch detailed for duty at No 6 Prisoners of War Camp BELLAVESNES.	
	3		Inspected billets at AGNEZ-les-DUISANS – advised that site of manure dump be altered to further away from billets	
	4		At Habarq 63rd Field Ambulance have made several improvements in the Sanitary arrangements there. The incinerator has been moved away from the wards & mens huts	
	5		Cpl Denny and L/Cpl Harding sent to Montenescourt for duty.	
	6		Inspected and reported on proposed Laundry at Rue St Pol AVESNES	
	7		Inspection of Sanitation at HAUTVILLE.	
	8		Visited ARRAS and made report on proposed bath house at No 2 Rue de Lille.	
	9		Inspected bath house at AGNEZ-les-DUISANS The building is of too temporary a nature for winter use I reported and recommended rebuilding and re-modelling.	
	10		At LOOEZ Laundry the heating arrangements in the drying rooms is very wasteful of fuel. Submitted recommendation for improving this.	
	11		Inspected Hutments in DUISANS – recommended that a cooks stove be built there – Saw case of GERMAN MEASLES in transport lines of 9th Liecester Regt.	
	12		At ARRAS went over work necessary at 2 RUE de LILLE for bath-house with O/c 97th ECo RE. Inspected Laundry of 110th Bde – Sgt Paul reported for Duty from Hospital.	
	13		Inspected Prisoners Camp at BELLAVESNES.	
	14		nil	
	15		Sgt Sutcliffe sent to WANIQUETIN to replace Sgt DEWHURST sent to 63rd FA	
	16		A bath house has now been erected at HABARQ.	
	17		RAMC Conference at VI Corps Headquarters	
	18		Inspected proposed Laundry at AVESNES with ADMS. +DAA QMG. – Motor Lorry sent to Div workshops for repair.	
	19		Routine duties	

O.C. SANITARY SECTION No 30
21st DIVISION.

WAR DIARY or INTELLIGENCE SUMMARY

Army Form C. 2118

August

Place	Date	Hour	Summary of Events and Information	Remarks and references to Appendices
DOISANS	20th		Inspected Sanitary Arrangements at HAUTVILLE. Work is done here now by German prisoners.	
	21st		Inspections in DOISANS. Drew attention of Town Major to fact that units were not all using the manure dump, but putting their manure in fields not under supervision.	
	22nd		Routine Duties	
	23rd		Inspected Sanitation of DAINVILLE and reported on same. Recommended that a new Bath-house be built.	
	24th		Inspected Sanitation at LATTRE ST QUENTIN, and reported. The sanitation in lines of 21st Div unit is satisfactory.	
	25th		Routine duties	
	26th		At LIGNEREUL 64th Field Amb. and inspected latrines and other sanitary appliances on exhibition there.	
	27th		Took over Carpenters shop from Town Major at DOISANS	
	28th		ROUTINE duties	
	29th		Disinfected clothing etc of convalescent civilian case of diphtheria at No 2 billet DOISANS; also disinfected billet of 2" Lt Orah VI Corps RE park who was removed to hospital suffering from Diphtheria.	
	30th		Routine duties	
	31st		Investigated suspected case of C.S.M. Pte LACK 65th Field Amb. This man's blood CSfluid & throat brushing was examined by bacteriologist at 37 CCS with negative result. No further action taken meantime.	

[signature]
O.C. SANITARY SECTION No. 38
21st DIVISION.

Sept 1916

140/1734

21st Div.

38th Sanitary Section

COMMITTEE FOR THE
MEDICAL HISTORY OF THE WAR
Date 30 OCT. 1916

WAR DIARY or **INTELLIGENCE SUMMARY**
(Erase heading not required.)

Army Form C. 2118

Instructions regarding War Diaries and Intelligence Summaries are contained in F.S. Regs., Part II. and the Staff Manual respectively. Title Pages will be prepared in manuscript.

Place	Date Sept 1916	Hour	Summary of Events and Information	Remarks and references to Appendices
DUISANS	1		Bath house at No. 2 RUE de LILLE ARRAS opened and Staff Captain of Brigades informed. The bath house will be run by a detachment from 65th Field Ambulance.	
	2		Went over sanitation of area with the OC San. Sect 35th Divn.	
	3		Advance party from 35th Divn San Sect. arrived at DUISANS and details of this party were sent to WANQUETIN, HAUTVILLE, MONTENESCOURT and AGNEZ-les-DUISANS	
	4		Inspected bathing arrangements in new area at Gd Rullecourt and BERLINCOURT.	
	5		Section moved to LE CAUROY.	
LE CAUROY	6		Inspected baths at BERLINCOURT which are being run for 110th Bde	
	7		Routine duties	
	8		Visited Baths in area and carried out general inspection.	
	9		Disinfected clothing sent to CAGNY laundry. Manager of laundry informs me that coal and labour must be supplied by Army. Sgt Dewhurst reported for duty from hospital	
	10		ROUTINE duties	
	11		Unit collected prior to marching out. Pte Jones left in charge at Berlincourt baths. Cpl Dutch reported for duty from Prisoners of War Camp BELLAVESNES	
LE CAUROY	12		Capt. Brown, appointed Pathologist to General Hosp. MARSEILLES, relinquishes his command of Sam Sec. Duties temporarily taken over by Capt. Holden - 64th Field Amb. - Half San. Sec. marched out with 65th Field Amb. to FRANCLEON - en route to BUIRE - Baths established at BERLINCOURT handed over to NCO. attached VI Corps	Jett
LE CAUROY / BUIRE	13th		21st Divl. H.Q. moved out to BUIRE. Capt. Brown departure for MARSEILLES - remainder of Sam Sec. with motor lorry departed for BUIRE - 10,000 pieces of dirty clothing dispatched in 3 motor lorries from LE CAUROY to CAGNY - Sgt Franklin in charge	Jett

PLACE	DATE	WAR DIARY
BUIRE	Sept 14th	Effected some improvements in Sanitation of H.Q. Camp at BUIRE - to AMIENS to interview manager of laundry - arrangements for obtaining clean clothing in short time rather precarious owing to five other Divisions using same laundry. J.C.H.
BUIRE	" 15th	Continued Sanitation of Camp. To AMIENS & interviewed Mons. PINCEDEZ re washing clothing for Division. Contribution this firm would be more satisfactory if arranged. J.C.H.
BUIRE	" 16th	Thresh Disinfector Foden lorry arrived from LECAUROY. As repairs are needed sent to 21st Divl. Supply Column Workshops whilst the Division are up in front. J.C.H.
BUIRE	" 17th	Divisional H.Q. moved up to FRICOURT CHATEAU CAMP - A squad & San. Sec. also sent up. Divisional Concert Party attached temporarily to San. Sec. for duties. J.C.H.
FRICOURT	" 18th	Remainder of San. Sec. & Divl. Concert Party moved into camp in neighbourhood of 21st Divl. H.Q. Lieut. JOHNSTONE - London Sanitary Company, reported his arrival & took over duties of Section Sanitary Officer.
Fricourt	" 19th	Lieut Johnstone commenced Duty as OC. Section; visited 64th Brigade Camp. Squad of 1 N.C.O + 10 men detailed for Sanitation at Divl. H.Q + to clean up dug-outs for occupation. W.J.
Fricourt	" 20	Continued Sanitation at H.Q. Details (Carpenters) from Divl Composite Company to make jackets boxes for Trench rations - W.J.
Fricourt	" 21	Made minute & detailed inspection of camp occupied by 64th Brigade. Found many defects including considerable shortage of water for ablution purposes; men washing in water collected in shell holes which in many cases was very foul. No incinerators & arrangements for disposal of urine unsatisfactory. Special report to A.D.M.S. W.J.

WAR DIARY or INTELLIGENCE SUMMARY

Army Form C. 2118

(Erase heading not required.)

Instructions regarding War Diaries and Intelligence Summaries are contained in F. S. Regs., Part II. and the Staff Manual respectively. Title Pages will be prepared in manuscript.

Place	Date 1916 Sept	Hour	Summary of Events and Information	Remarks and references to Appendices
Fricourt	22	—	64th Brigade moved out of Camp: 62nd BRIGADE come in. Camp in disordered & filthy state. Full strength of Sanitary Section put on to clean up & the South Latrines which require changing.	W.J.
"	23	—	Incinerator begun previous evening dismantled by incoming troops 62nd Brigade. The camp is still unsatisfactory from a sanitary point of view chiefly owing to lack of transport & fatigue to clean up thoroughly. Ablution problem still unsolved. Sanitary section at work all day.	W.J.
"	24	—	Sanitation of 62nd Brigade Camp (incint) continued. 6 G.S. wagons sent to assist in removing rubbish to definite areas. Lines somewhat cleaner. 8 men under N.C.O. detailed to bury 4 horses in A.V.C. lines.	W.J.
"	25	—	Carpentering of trench boxes finished. Instructions given to carpenters to make some ablution benches & urine troughs for camp also painting of notices "foul ground" &c to mark definite spots in camp area.	W.J.
"	26	—	1 N.C.O. & 4 men detailed for sanitary work at advanced H.Q. Montauban:— Work continued at Brigade Camp. BÉCORDEL	W.J.
"	27	—	Inspected Advanced HQ Camp at MONTAUBAN. 4 Latrine boxes sent for emplacement. Rubbish lying about buried.	W.J.
"	28	—	1st Guards Brigade now occupy lines at Brigade Camp BÉCORDEL. Sanitary section work completed and lines left in good sanitary condition. 7 horses killed by enemy shell fire buried at Div'l HQ Fricourt. Lines occupied by 64th F.A. at S 23.a.47 inspected; considerable amount of excreta found in shell holes	W.J. Wm Johnstone

WAR DIARY ~~INTELLIGENCE SUMMARY~~

Army Form C. 2118

(Erase heading not required.)

Place	Date Sept 1916	Hour	Summary of Events and Information	Remarks and references to Appendices
Fricourt	29	—	Section detailed for sanitary duty at Advanced dressing Station MONTAUBAN-LONGUEVAL road at S23.a 4.7. Six Latrine boxes erected and trench dug. 1 N.C.O. & 2 men detailed for water duty at water points FRICOURT. Taken over from 55th Division.	6.7
"	30	—	Routine Sanitary Duties.	

Wm Johnstone
O.C. SANITARY SECTION
21st DIVISION.

Oct. 1916

140/181

21st Div.

38th Sanitary Section

COMMITTEE FOR THE
MEDICAL HISTORY OF THE WAR
Date -9 DEC. 1916

WAR DIARY or INTELLIGENCE SUMMARY

(Erase heading not required.)

Army Form C. 2118

MEDICAL

Instructions regarding War Diaries and Intelligence Summaries are contained in F. S. Regs., Part II. and the Staff Manual respectively. Title Pages will be prepared in manuscript.

Place	Date 1916 Oct.	Hour	Summary of Events and Information	Remarks and references to Appendices
FRICOURT	1	—	Advance party sent to BUIRE Camp.	W.J.
BUIRE	2	—	Remainder of section moved to BUIRE. NCO + men on duty at water points FRICOURT relieved by details from Sanitary Section 12th Division.	W.J.
"	3	—	Inspection of BUIRE Divl. HQ Camp + men detailed for any sanitary duties required. Section evacuated BUIRE Camp + with Divl. concert party entrained for AILLY LE HT CLOCHER via LONGPRÉ. Foden Thresh taken by road from HEILLY.	W.J.
AILLY LE HT CLOCHER	4	—	Arrived LONGPRÉ 1 a.m. Billeted in barn overnight. Marched to AILLY LE HT CLOCHER this morning. Sketches of sites of various sanitary arrangements including Weir's tent by DADMS 24th Division gave valuable information.	W.J.
"	5	—	Routine Sanitary duties undertaken.	W.J.
"	6	—	Sanitary duties continued.	W.J.
"	7	—	Transport arrangements for movement to new area completed. In addition 1 N.C.O. + 6 men taken to laundry at CAGNY to expedite Divl. washing	W.J.
"	8	7 a.m. 10.30 p.m.	Section moved from AILLY LE HT CLOCHER to entrain at ABBEVILLE. Detrainment at CHOCQUES railhead for NOEUX LES MINES.	W.J.
NOEUX-LES-MINES	9	12.30 a.m.	Arrived in new area. Sanitary arrangements in hands of Town Major who has P.B. men for fatigues. N.C.O. told off to report to Town Major to get exact information as to sanitary arrangements.	W.J.
"	10	—	Sanitary duties continued in NOEUX-LES-MINES.	W.J.
SAILLY-LABOURSE	11	—	21st Division officially takes over from 8th Divn. 14th Sanitary Section left charts showing appliances in various villages of area. There are baths in running order at LABOURSE (Tubs), SAILLY-LABOURSE (Sprays), NOYELLES (Sprays), FOUQUIERES (Sprays), VERMELLES (Tubs).	W.J.
	12	—	21 P.B. men are attached Sanitary Section for duties which in addition to ordinary work includes collection of civilians + billet refuse in SAILLY LABOURSE + conveyance to public incinerator. There is a good workshop in LABOURSE in which work 2 NCOs of Sanitary Section + 2 men of Composite Coy. making sanitary appliances.	W.J.

WAR DIARY or INTELLIGENCE SUMMARY

Army Form C. 2118

(Erase heading not required.)

Place	Date 1916 Oct.	Hour	Summary of Events and Information	Remarks and references to Appendices
SAILLY-LABOURSE	13	—	Sanitary work in SAILLY, LABOURSE & other villages in area. Insufficient transport for satisfactory collection of refuse in SAILLY & LABOURSE. 65th F.A. supplied two G.S. wagons temporarily.	W.J.
"	14	—	2½ Division took over a Brigade area from 32nd Div. including ANNEQUIN and CAMBRIN. Chart of Sanitary arrangements in ANNEQUIN supplied by Sanitary Section of that Div. General Sanitary arrangements are satisfactory as regards number of conveniences but many bucket latrines require replacing by deep trench latrines & a few near HQ (Bgde) were not very clean. There is a good set of Spray baths in ANNEQUIN capable of bathing 500-600 men per diem.	W.J.
"	15	—	Made complete inspection of Sanitary arrangements in NOYELLES and FOUQUIÈRES. In the former village occupied by 14th N.F. & 3rd Field Coy RE, everything was satisfactory. There are too many bucket latrines in FOUQUIÈRES entailing an unnecessary amount of labour in emptying.	W.J.
"	16	—	Reports on Examination of water from pumps in SAILLY & LABOURSE show it to be satisfactory. Chlorination figure is "1" in all cases where supply for drinking is marked.	W.J.
"	17	—	Set (complete) of Spray baths (6) for erection at new bathhouse, 110th Brigade VERMELLES taken from D.S.C. Nuisance from cesspool at Divl HQ rectified by cleaning out & having Call-a put in.	W.J.
"	18	—	Lines of 33rd Battery R.F.A., 1st Lincolns Transport, LABOURSE inspected. Latrines satisfactory in number & condition. Billets in lofts of former unit satisfactory on whole. Too much standing water. Made complete inspection of VERMELLES; certain renovations & alterations required & asked, also sheds require building over certain latrines.	W.J.
"	19	—	Carried out tour of inspection of FOUQUIÈRES, VERQUIGNEUL and ANNEQUIN. At FOUQUIÈRES a latrine used by Officers of Divl Train A.S.C. requires dismantling & another box seat added to adjacent latrine. Sacking round certain latrines & urinals dilapidated & requires renewal also receptacles for sanitary paper to be provided in every case. 3 cases of infectious disease reported all amongst civilians in area of Division. One enteric (suspected) and one Diphtheria at LZOSS and a diphtheria case at ANNEQUIN (Billet 30). [Houses have been put out of bounds in all cases] 8th Divl D.A.C. still occupy lines at VERQUIGNEUL.	W.J.
"	20	—	Disinfection carried out by formalin spraying in houses occupied by cases of infectious diseases amongst civilians in area notified yesterday. Have drawn up scheme of concentrated sanitary effort to improve matters at VERMELLES. 200 blankets from 97th R.F. disinfected in Thresh to-day.	W.J.

WAR DIARY or INTELLIGENCE SUMMARY

Army Form C. 2118.

(Erase heading not required).

Place	Date 1915 Oct.	Hour	Summary of Events and Information	Remarks and references to Appendices
SAILLY-LABOURSE	21	—	Sanitary structures erected at VERMELLES and Spray bath set completed at 110th Brigade bath house.	W.J.
"	22	—	Visited trenches: CAMBRIN and HOHENZOLLERN Sectors — Recommendations made to responsible authorities in each as to certain minor improvements.	W.J.
"	23	—	Inspected trenches QUARRIES Sector. Latrines chiefly situated in O.B.1. mostly trench, some odd cases buckets, one or two of which had not been emptied. Staff Sgt. (Sanitary) accompanying informed.	W.J.
"	24	—	Consultation with Staff Capt. 62nd Brigade re erecting sprays in present bathhouse at VERMELLES	W.J.
"	25	—	Routine inspections at LABOURSE, SAILLY, VERMELLES, ANNEQUIN, also certain billets (18,19,37,102) in LABOURSE. N.C.Os i/c baths NOYELLES & ANNEQUIN replaced by N.C.O from 7A.	W.J.
"	26	—	Visited Divl. School FERFAY. Left N.C.O. & 3 RAMC details to take charge of baths at BELLERY. Made inspection of Chateau grounds with Lieut. Low R.E. — Suggested improvements, alterations & fresh erections to make Sanitation generally more satisfactory. Report given to ADMS.	} W.J.
"	27	—	Routine inspection of DAC lines VERQUIGNEUL. New grease trap put into position behind Bathhouse ANNEQUIN. Spray bath apparatus dismantled at NOYELLES & taken to VERMELLES.	W.J.
"	28	—	Carried out investigation into alleged verminous condition of underclothing supplied from laundry to ANNEQUIN baths — No live adults or eggs found. Report on this subject to ADMS. Arranged with O.C. 14 NF(P) Coy. at ANNEQUIN to erect partition for ironing room at baths.	W.J.
"	29	—	Consultation with O.C. 97th Field Coy RE regarding erection of sprays at VERMELLES and alterations required to give necessary accommodation for 62nd Bgde baths.	W.J.
"	30	—	At ANNEQUIN bathhouse Supervised putting in proper filter to grease trap. Visited trenches 62nd Bgde up to O.B.1.	W.J.
"	31	—	Inspected general sanitation of NOYELLES & billets 92-99. Overcrowding in billet 99. Town Major informed for necessary action — Site for new latrine for these billets selected.	W.J.

Wm Johnstone Capt.
O.C. 38 Sanitary Section 1. Divn.

Nov. 1916

21st Div.

140/1943

38th Sanitary Section

COMMITTEE FOR THE
MEDICAL HISTORY OF THE WAR
Date 13 MAR. 1917

WAR DIARY or INTELLIGENCE SUMMARY

Army Form C. 2118.

38 Sanitary ~~MEDICAL~~

Vol 15

Place	Date Nov 1916	Hour	Summary of Events and Information	Remarks and references to Appendices
SAILLY LABOURSE	1	—	Routine Sanitary duties.	
	2	a.m.	Visited trenches with M.O. 1st E. Yorks to inspect defects in factory Trench CAMBRIN sector. Report to ADMS.	
		p.m.	Made complete tour of inspection into Sanitary arrangements at VERMELLES. Disused latrines have been filled in & 3 new sets erected also new urinals & reconstructed incinerator.	
	3	—	Inspected LABOURSE throughout – including Transport Lines of 6th & 7th Leicesters. Improvements & alterations undertaken. Visited ANNEQUIN.	
	4	—	R.E. have started reconstructing VERMELLES bathhouse 62nd Brigade, concreting floor and timbering ironing & dressing rooms – Sanitary Section assisting.	
	5	—	Improvements to NOYELLES baths & yard undertaken – Sanitation generally of NOYELLES Satisfactory. Fresh receptacles being made at workshop for better refuse disposal at NOYELLES.	
	6	—	Inspected ANNEQUIN in its entirety. Latrine buildings very unsatisfactory. Refuse disposal has been almost nil – many tins lying about & several broken down incinerators.	
	7	—	Concentrated effort on ANNEQUIN. Bad weather hindered operations materially. Interviewed Town Major regarding selection of site for dump & O.C. A Coy 4th N.F. (P)R.E. constructional work at baths. Arranged for ironing of tunics & trousers at LABOURSE baths, each man of batch being butted to do his own – Tour of wells at VERMELLES with Sergt. 97th R.E. Pumps No. 3 & at 3 Bomb Store to be put in working order. Sanitation of 62nd Brigade H.Q. inspected.	
	8	—	Consultation with O.C. Laundry regarding ironing arrangements at Baths & programme of inspection daily. Made Sanitary inspection of VERQUIGNEUL determining sites for 3 public latrines.	
	9	—	Visited VERMELLES to speed up opening of 62nd Bgde baths. Constructional work practically finished. Obtained advice of O.C. 97th Coy R.E. regarding advisability of making use of Wells No. 3 & 9. These we found to be deep wells with bore tubes & therefore worth repairing. Well at Tower Keep open. Visited trenches – ? new supply at CHAPEL KEEP Tube of former well found. No water at 12ft. Inspected O.B.4 water supply. Pump in dug out – Many latrine buckets in OBT not emptied. No orderly at Gordon Alley water-point. Tanks kempt. – Report on above to ADMS.	
	10	—	Visited FOUQUIERES, FOUQUEREUIL & Town Major at ANNEZIN. Units of 6th Divn only in FOUQUEREUIL	
		p.m.	ANNEQUIN (Baths) & NOYELLES (baths) to inspect ironing arrangements. Not satisfactory in NOYELLES.	

WAR DIARY or INTELLIGENCE SUMMARY

Army Form C. 2118.

(Erase heading not required).

Place	1916 Date Nov	Hour	Summary of Events and Information	Remarks and references to Appendices
SAILLY-LABOURSE	11	—	Visited Divl Laundry BETHUNE re irregularities in Programme at Baths — Inspected Clayton Fumigator at 24th Divl Laundry — Inspected SAILLY-LABOURSE throughout. Arranged baths programme NOYELLES & VERMELLES — units bathing on Sunday.	
	12	—	Inspected sanitation of NOYELLES with Town Major. Similarly improvements at ANNEQUIN.	
	13	—	Instructed 14 NF (Pioneers) NCO regarding alterations for new ironing room at NOYELLES. Work begun. Arranged with T.M. SAILLY re 4 civilian women to start work as ironers at LABOURSE baths.	
	14	—	Routine sanitary duties in LABOURSE — Undertook inquiry into alleged increasing verminous condition of men in 62nd Bde early B-G. Satisfied him by personal visit to 62nd Baths VERMELLES that systematic ironing was being done to meet this difficulty.	
	15	—	Interviewed O.C. 97th F.C. RE regarding the laying of a drain from bathhouse to prevent possibility of flooding of A.D.S. — Work begun. Ironing room at NOYELLES Baths practically completed. 62nd Bde VERMELLES.	
	16	—	Attended conference of ADMS & OsC San Secs of Divisions comprising 1st Corps. Working conclusive. Went to lecture on Sanitation at Divl School FERFAY. Arranged with O/C No. 6 Mob Lab. Unit for samples of water for analysis re to be taken on 18/11/16.	
	17	—	Visited trenches: sanitation of VILLAGE LINE, GORDON ALLEY, & 110th Bgde HQ HULLUCH ALLEY.	
	18	a.m.	VERMELLES for water samples pumps 3 & 7. Report on pump 3, "water grossly contaminated".	
		p.m.	VERQUIGNEUL, investigation into two civilian cases of Rabies — Report forwarded to ADMS.	
	19	—	Inspected LABOURSE in its entirety — Water sample taken from pump at billet 40. Parade and Kit inspection of whole section.	
	20	—	Visited VERMELLES to take water sample from new pump (7a) for analysis & inspected water cart belonging to 62nd M.G.C. — Reported on this to ADMS. NOYELLES & ANNEQUIN Town Majors interviewed regarding employment of women as "ironers" at baths.	
	21	—	FOUQUIÈRES inspected — Incinerators require repairing — This place is mostly occupied by details from 6th Division — Interviewed O.C. San Sec 6th Divn regarding proposed retiring of bathhouse by this Divn.	

WAR DIARY or INTELLIGENCE SUMMARY

Army Form C. 2118.

Place	Date Nov. 1916	Hour	Summary of Events and Information	Remarks and references to Appendices
SAILLY-LABOURSE	22	a.m.	VERMELLES, NOYELLES and ANNEQUIN visited chiefly in relation to bathing arrangements.	
		p.m.	Sanitation of NOYELLES inspected in its entirety. Much need for improvement all round especially with reference to refuse behind billets 94-99 and sanitary state of Chateau.	
	23	—	Reconstructional work proceeding at ANNEQUIN – Inspected 64th Bgde HQ + gun emplacements RFA. Certain alterations required at Bgde HQ south ANNEQUIN.	
	24	—	Monthly sanitary report completed & forwarded ADMS. q.v. for improvements carried out by Sanitary Section during previous month. Visited 74th F.A. *LABEUVRIÈRE* under instructions to see iron-heater made out of oil drum. Not favourably impressed!	
	25	—	Routine sanitary inspections NOYELLES & ANNEQUIN. Improvements being carried out in both places.	
	26	—	Suggested site for public incinerator in SAILLY to deal with Trench Refuse at L.3.6.7.4. also inspected SAILLY-LABOURSE in its entirety (including Divl. HQ at Chateau). +QMS &13th N.F. Several improvements indicated.	
	27	—	Made tour of inspection of NOYELLES and VERQUIGNEUL. New public latrine erected in latter at F.25.c.3.0. – Brick grease trap being erected behind ANNEQUIN bathhouse (4 compartment combined downward & upward filtration). Gave orders that latrines throughout Divl area must be numbered (a) in series (b) according to number of seats thus 1/5, 2/3 &c.	
	28	.	Visited Trenches, Quarries Sector chiefly. Took two samples of water from (a) Gordon pump (b) Junction Keep ("Springwell"). Went up HULLUCH ALLEY, Stansfield Road, to OBT. Found sanitation of the [improved]	
	29	—	Inspected A.& D. Well Lain FOURVIERES. No 1 Coy. incinerator broken – to be repaired forthwith – No 2 Coy are building new latrine of their own, & inspected one or two billets with M.O. also water cart (No 2 Coy.) – Too many CaOCl₂ tins, some water in box & spares wanting.	
		p.m.	Inspected Tobacco factory & Orphanage BETHUNE. Report to ADMS. Had interview with O.C. San Sec 6th Divn. with a view to taking over billets in BEULER JEUNE FOSSE.	
	30	—	CAMBRIN Sector, including ANNEQUIN, taken over by San Sec 6th Division. For improvements carried out in ANNEQUIN see separate report.	

Wm Johnstone Capt.
O.C. 38 San Sec 2 War

Dec 1916.

21st Div.

140/1943

38th Sanitary Section.

COMMITTEE FOR THE
MEDICAL HISTORY OF THE WAR
Date   13 MAR. 1917

WAR DIARY or INTELLIGENCE SUMMARY

Army Form C. 2118.

(Erase heading not required).

Place	Date 1916 Dec	Hour	Summary of Events and Information	Remarks and references to Appendices
SAILLY-LABOURSE	1	—	Visited trenches chiefly HOHENZOLLERN SECTOR. BARTS ALLEY, QUARRY ALLEY; KEEPS, Railway trench.	
"	2	—	Sanitary inspection of billets & surroundings occupied by 64th Bgde troops in BETHUNE. Arrangements made with 5th Division re baths at École de Jeune Filles taken over 30.XI.16	
"	3	a.m.	Inspected LABOURSE throughout. Latrine (Officers & NCOs) required Rue Nouex-les-Mines Road.	
		p.m.	" MONTMORENCY Barracks, BETHUNE — Report on sanitary defects to ADMS.	
"	4	—	Visited and made tour of NOYELLES, also billets occupied by 1st E. Yorks & 13th NF in PHILOSOPHE & MAZINGARBE.	
"	5	—	AT VERMELLES — Completed drinking water arrangements by erecting apparatus at 110th Bgde baths. Interviewed Staff Capt re alterations at dressing room for disposal dirty clothing at bathhouse, 110th Bgde.	
"	6	—	Delivered lecture on Sanitation at 21st Divl School FERFAY and interviewed Col Mears re FOUQUIERES bath arrangements.	
"	7	—	Visited trenches and made plan of sanitary arrangements in QUARRY ALLEY, inspected QUARRY pump. Suggested alterations behind BARTS ALLEY (commencement), CENTRAL KEEP, CANNON St. RESERVE TRENCH. OBT	
"	8	—	Routine sanitary duties in SAILLY and SAILLY-LABOURSE.	
"	9	—	Sent special report to Staff Capt 62nd Bgde for remedy of sanitary defects in their trench area found on 7th. Inspected VERMELLES with NCO's.	
"	10	—	Interview with O.C. San Sec 24th Div at PHILOSOPHE re complaint against 1st E. Yorks recently billeted there. Inspected MONTMORENCY Barracks, and Tobacco Factory BETHUNE with Town Sanitary Officer BETHUNE & Town Major.	
"	11	—	Inspected sanitation of NOYELLES with NCO's. This shows considerable improvement.	
"	12	—	do. FOUQUIERES. 6th Div. having vacated. Visited all transport lines in SAILLY and neighbourhood including 15th D.L.I, DAC &c.	
"	13	—	Made complete tour of LABOURSE — Complaint that 203rd (T) Coy not doing wiring at baths and bucket latrine behind Officers' mess not satisfactory — Report to ADMS.	

Wm Johnstone Capt
O.C. SANITARY SECTION
21st DIVISION

WAR DIARY or INTELLIGENCE SUMMARY

(Erase heading not required).

Army Form C. 2118.

Place	Date 1916 Dec	Hour	Summary of Events and Information	Remarks and references to Appendices
SAILLY-LABOURSE	14	—	Made tour of inspection in trenches including BART'S ALLEY (commencement), GORDON ALLEY (up to 160.0) VILLAGE LINE, JUNCTION KEEP, STANSFIELD ROAD, CURLEY CRESCENT, OB5, OB4, CHAPEL ALLEY &c. Found sanitation of trenches much improved, new latrine boxes & trough urinals erected in above sites.	
"	15	—	Inspected FOUQUIÈRES district & lines occupied by 21st Divl train and Divl batts. Handed over Battns at College jeune fille, BETHUNE to O.C. 14th Field Amb[ulance] representing 5th Div[ision]. Conference with D.D.M.S. at NOEUX-LES-MINES re making San. Sec[tion] army troops.	
"	16	—	Tour of inspection in DAC lines VERQUIGNEUL. Certain recommendations made to Town Major re improvements.	
"	17	—	Routine sanitary duties and inspection in SAILLY & LABOURSE. Incinerator at HARFORD ROAD, SAILLY & well head at billet 33 require cementing. Inquiry into alleged nuisance at billet 103. Report to Town Major.	
"	18	—	NOYELLES, general inspection of lines including R.E. RFA, 14 NF (Pioneers).	
"	19	—	Routine inspection of VERMELLES, and bathhouses at NOYELLES and VERMELLES.	
"	20	—	Tour of trenches both HOHENZOLLERN and QUARRIES SECTORS. Notes & sketches of necessary improvements.	
"	21	—	General inspection re alleged nuisance and requirements in SAILLY & LABOURSE.	
"	22	—	Visited D.H.Q. Chateau SAILLY. Arranged billets in new area with Camp Comm[andan]t. Gave orders to Workshop to start making for new area at once — NOEUX-LES-MINES battns & T.M.	
"	23	—	Certain parts of new area visited.	
"	24	—	FOUQUIÈRES, LABEUVRIERE to inspect Chateau de Sars, arrange for billets & workshop for section, also 110th Bgd. H.Q. at AUCHEL. Stock of clothing & personnel required for baths at RAIMBERT.	
"	25	—	Xmas day.	

Wm Johnstone
Capt
O.C. SANITARY SECTION
21st DIVISION.

WAR DIARY or INTELLIGENCE SUMMARY

(Erase heading not required).

Army Form C. 2118.

Sanit. Sec
21 Div
Vol 16

Place	Date Dec. 1916	Hour	Summary of Events and Information	Remarks and references to Appendices
SAILLY-LABOURSE	26	—	Made tour of Divisional area with O.C. 8th San. Sec 6th Divn. preparatory to handing over.	
	27	—	Preliminaries for move to new area — Visited LABEUVRIÈRE to arrange billets	
LABEUVRIÈRE	28	—	Moved officially into this area. Practically no Sanitary appliances at LAPUGNOY, AUCHEL, RAIMBERT, ALLOUAGNE, LOZINGHEM, CAUCHY-A LA TOUR, & insufficient at LABEUVRIÈRE.	
"	29	—	Visited FOUQUIÈRES & FOUQUEREUIL, also CALONNE-RICOUART baths at Mine 1 & 7.1. With D.A.D.M.S. No baths at ALLOUAGNE to be found.	
"	30	—	Inspected LAPUGNOY — 14th N.F.(P) have no proper latrines — 1st Lincs are similarly circumstanced at LOZINGHEM, as also 12th N.F. at ALLOUAGNE. No incinerators in these latter communes. 6-seater public latrine erected in Petite Place, LABEUVRIÈRE.	
"	31	—	Inspected 9th Leicesters' area at RAIMBERT. Found similar deficiency in Sanitary arrangements. Interviewed Staff Capt 110th Bgde with reference to necessity of establishing a Brigade Workshop in AUCHEL to make latrines &c for whole Brigade area.	

Remarks:

The sanitation of this area, with the possible exception of LABEUVRIÈRE is as unsatisfactory as it can possibly be. Brigades and units of this Division on moving in found that there were no sanitary conveniences of any description for their men — not even a public latrine.

To cope with this deficiency it is proposed to establish Brigade workshops at AUCHEL (110th) and ALLOUAGNE (62nd), but the supply of suitable timber on advice of the Divl. R.E. being limited, the work of making districts occupied by our troops satisfactory from a sanitary point of view will be of necessity greatly hampered.

Wm Johnstone
Capt. O.C. SANITARY SECTION
21st DIVISION

Jan. 1917

21st Div.

140/1943.

38th Sanitary Section.

COMMITTEE FOR THE
MEDICAL HISTORY OF THE WAR
Date 13 MAR. 1917

WAR DIARY or INTELLIGENCE SUMMARY

Army Form C. 2118.
3¼ Sanitary ~~MEDICAL~~
Vol 17

Place	Date	Hour	Summary of Events and Information	Remarks and references to Appendices
LABEUVRIÈRE	Jan 1917 1	—	Inspected FOUQUIÈRES district & baths. Interviewed M.O. 1st E. Yorks who reports sanitation satisfactory. Staff Capts 62nd & 110th Bgde approached re establishing workshops to make sanitary material for respective areas. Visited 1st Corps HQ to interview Field Engineer re better sanitation of ALLOUAGNE.	
"	2	a.m. / p.m.	Interviewed C.R.E. LAPUGNOY on question of adequate supplies of timber for latrines to workshops at ALLOUAGNE & AUCHEL. Interviewed Field Engineer 1st Corps and arranged to have timber from his yard at ALLOUAGNE to stock 62nd Bgde workshop. This was done & work started.	
"	3	—	110th Bgde workshop stocked with timber & started at AUCHEL. Baths at RAIMBERT inspected re ironing. Visited CALONNE baths – arrangements as to storage of clothing & billeting arrangements of personnel unsatisfactory. 13th N.F. HQ at MARLES-LES-MINES. Workshop at ALLOUAGNE has turned out 5 seater latrine complete with shed also 3 seater with base. AUCHEL Workshops also visited.	
"	4	—	Routine sanitary inspections generally in LAPUGNOY & Tile works LABEUVRIÈRE for DADOS.	
"	5	—	To CAGNY to settle a/c at Deveux Frères laundry for Divn on 6"/10 & 12"/10 – Informed that of 9522 a shirts remaining at least 1/3 will be unserviceable. To be informed later of exact statistics. Carpenters to FOUQUIÈRES to repair 2 latrines. Urinal erected Petite Place, LABEUVRIÈRE, also ablution benches erected for Ordnance in tile works. Further supplies timber drawn from R.E. & supplies taken to ALLOUAGNE.	
"	6	—	Inspected AUCHEL, RAIMBERT, CAUCHY A LA TOUR in their entirety. Found 6th Leicesters had made satisfactory box seat latrines. Other units of 110th Bgde had not made same progress. Much work still requires to be done in these communes. Also visited AUCHEL & RAIMBERT baths. Ironing reported being carried out.	
"	7	—	Two carpenters from San. Sec. Workshop detailed for 110th Bgde Pioneer Workshop to speed up sanitary constructional work. Inspected ALLOUAGNE, 3 new 5 seater latrines erected for 12th N.F. Visited BURBURE. R.F.A. battery there. Sanitation as defective as in other parts.	
"	8	—	C.R.E. LAPUGNOY for further supplies of timber & material. Interviewed M.O. battery 95th Bgde R.F.A. & made tour of inspection of ECQUEDECQUES. Sanitary improvements suggested & material for same to be sent out.	
"	9	—	Repairs carried out to damaged latrines at FOUQUIÈRES – Material taken to MARLES-LES-MINES to 13th N.F. sufficient to make two 6-seater latrines – Material drawn from R.E. yard.	

Wm Johnstone Capt.

WAR DIARY or INTELLIGENCE SUMMARY

(Erase heading not required)

Army Form C. 2118.

Instructions regarding War Diaries and Intelligence Summaries are contained in F. S. Regs., Part II, and the Staff Manual respectively. Title Pages will be prepared in manuscript.

Place	Date Jan 1917	Hour	Summary of Events and Information	Remarks and references to Appendices
LABEUVRIÈRE	10	-	Brigade Sanitary work continued and material for carrying on conveyed to various areas. Constructional work at San Sec workshop also continued.	
"	11	-	To 95th R.F.A. ECQUEDECQUES 10 Latrine seats, Timber, canvas, 110 Latrine buckets sufficient for two latrines.	
"	12	-	District Sanitation maintained progress. Rather more material (ration boxes) available for latrines.	
"	13	-	NCO at AUCHEL reports new constructional work by section carpenters there as follows:- (1) Roofing & screening of Latrine at 110th Bgde HQ (2) 4 Seater Latrine erected at gymnasium attached (3) 2 Seater for 110th T.M.B. (4) New 4-seat in hand at site selected as necessary by Town Major.	
"	14	-	Incinerators erected at R.E. stores 1st LINCS, LOZINGHEM. Material taken to MARLES, & AUCHEL for RIMBERT. Incineration reported urgently required for various communes in Div. area. No corrugated iron available from R.E.	
"	15	-	CAUCHY à la TOUR occupied by 8th Leicesters has now 15 Latrines & 5 urinals but many of these are deficient in screening and sheds. More material (12 latrine boxes) taken to MARLES for 10th Yorks also 1. 5-seat latrine to AUCHEL for RIMBERT.	
"	16	-	More material supplied to 62nd & 110th Brigades workshops for making of further new structures.	
"	17	-	Reports of NCOs at AUCHEL & ALLOUAGNE. Incinerators reported sufficient at ALLOUAGNE for burning of refuse which is brought by Sanitary personnel of each Coy. 12th N.F. Two seater men's + one officers latrines erected for use of "working party" 12th N.F.	
"	18	-	Two incinerators erected at LOZINGHEM for 1st Lincolns making a total of four there.	
"	19	-	To FOUQUIÈRES, 5 latrine seats for buckets (no 2 latrine). To MARLES-LES-MINES, 12 boxes for 10th Yorks. Regt. 62nd Bgde.	

Wm Johnstone Capt.

WAR DIARY
or
INTELLIGENCE SUMMARY
(Erase heading not required).

Army Form C. 2118.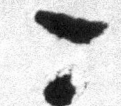

Place	Date Jan 1917	Hour	Summary of Events and Information	Remarks and references to Appendices
LABEUVRIÈRE	20	-	Inspected sanitation of communes of LOZINGHEM where sheds are much required for latrines but have not been erected for lack of material: ALLOUAGNE wh: seems satisfactory; LAPUGNOY & LABEUVRIÈRE where a new 4-seater has been erected in the Rue de GOSNAY for 6th Divn details billeted there.	
"	21	-	Visited MARLES-LES-MINES where 13th N.F. & 10th Yorks are. Sanitation of latter is fairly good. Interviewed M.O. 13th N.Fs. on subject of improving that of his unit. New 5-seater and canvas for screening supplied to him on request. Trenches have not been dug deep enough.	
"	22	-	Examined ALLOUAGNE in its entirety; proceeded to BURBURE & ECQUEDECQUES. Two new 5-seater bucket latrines erected there for 95th Bgde R.F.A. — not sufficient. Latrines at BURBURE very primitive & absence of incinerators noteworthy. Interviewed M.O. 10th KOYLI at FOUQUEREUIL & inspected billets occupied (case of German measles). Recommended remaining 13 men to be put in fresh billets & infected one disinfected. Inspected FOUQUIÈRES — public incinerator (brick) demolished & corrugated iron one in its place.	
"	23	-	Appointment with O.C. 41st San Sec 24th Divn to go over his area with view to taking over.	
"	24	-	Made routine inspections of AUCHEL & CAUCHY with NCOR. More sheds for latrines wanted at CAUCHY. Minx RE to arrange supplies of bricks for incinerators at ECQUEDECQUES. Saw baths at HOUCHIN.	
"	25	-	To FÉRFAY, 21st Divl School; lecture on Sanitation. Visited ECQUEDECQUES with ADMS to arrange improvements in sanitation for training battalion to be stationed there. Interviewed C.O. of same. NCOs at AUCHEL & ALLOUAGNE brigade areas instructed to return to HQ with their men.	
"	26	-	Advance party of 4 NCOs sent to BRACQUEMONT & LES BREBIS respectively to learn details of working of these places & neighbouring communes by 41st San. Sec. 24th Divn.	
"	27	-	Orders for move into 24th Divl area cancelled. Withdrew NCOs sent yesterday to BRACQUEMONT & LES BREBIS preparatory to moving elsewhere.	

Wm Johnstone
Capt.

WAR DIARY or INTELLIGENCE SUMMARY

Army Form C. 2118

Instructions regarding War Diaries and Intelligence Summaries are contained in F. S. Regs., Part II. and the Staff Manual respectively. Title Pages will be prepared in manuscript.

(Erase heading not required.)

Place	Date Jan 1917	Hour	Summary of Events and Information	Remarks and references to Appendices
	28	-	Ten sketch maps of FOUQUIERES, FOUQUEREUIL, LABEUVRIÈRE, LAPUGNOY, MARLES-LES-MINES, AUCHEL, RAIMBERT, CAUCHY à la TOUR, ALLOUAGNE, FLOZIINGHEM showing sites of sanitary appliances in each transmitted to DDMS, 1st Corps for disposal, no sanitary section taking over that area for the present. Section moved with the Division to WORMHOUDT.	
WORMHOUDT	29	-	Disinfection of Stables at Divl HQ carried out by advice of ADVS.	
"	30	-	Preliminary tour of WORMHOUDT. Difficulty in obtaining billets for personnel of section. Office procured at Estaminet au DAMEN, C.17. a. o. g. Sheet 27 1:40,000. Proceeded to AIRE to have lorry repaired at Tyre press ASC. ISBESQUES.	
"	31	-	Two seater Latrine and urinal erected at Divl HQ WORMHOUDT. Incinerator still required.	

Wm Johnstone
Capt.
O.C. SANITARY SECTION
21st DIVISION.

Feb. 1917.   21st Div   140/99/1

38th Sanitary Section.

COMMITTEE FOR THE
MEDICAL HISTORY OF THE W..
Date   4 - APR. 1917

WAR DIARY or INTELLIGENCE SUMMARY

Army Form C. 2118

Sanitary Sec 21 D.
MEDICAL

Vol 18

Place	Date Feb 1917	Hour	Summary of Events and Information	Remarks and references to Appendices
WORMHOUDT	1	a.m.	With Town Major, WORMHOUDT, sites were selected for Officer's and men's latrines Rue De PROGRES, also site for auxiliary incinerator – Work continued at D.H.Q.	
		p.m.	Visited 62nd Bgde area in A16 Sheet 28 Ref. Map. Inspected 12th NF, 10th Yorks, +1st Lincs lines – Incinerator ground in 1st Lincs lines quite with accumulation of ashtins & refuse. Interviewed Staff Capt. 62nd Bgde on subject of bathing arrangements for the Bngde.	
"	2	–	To HOUTKERQUE to arrange if sites for baths for 110th Bgde could be procured. Site selected in the Brasserie HOUTKERQUE; also arranged with O.C. baths at HERZEELE for use of 55th Div. baths there. At POPERINGHE, 39th Div. new baths capable of bathing 120 per hour. This can be used for baths 62nd Bgde. Detachments of Sanitary Section sent out to 62nd & 110th Bgde areas. 64th Bgde area worked from D.H.Q	
"	3	–	New latrine erected in Rue d'Eglise WORMHOUT (3 seater). Officers urinal put up in Grand Place do. – Site selected & trench dug for latrine in Rue du Progrés. Made attempt to find suitable place for 64th Bgde baths. Salt refinery in WORMHOUDT finally agreed upon.	
"	4	–	N.C.O's re WORMHOUDT, HOUTKERQUE (110th Bgde area) report sanitary arrangements quite inadequate in all these areas. Structures very crude & primitive. Marked absence of incinerators. Corrision incinerator erected at billet of 21st Signals RE, WORMHOUDT-DUNKIRK Rd.	
"	5	–	2 NCOs to HERZEELE with clothing to run baths – Inspected Sanitation of 9th & 8th Leicesters HOUTKERQUE district & KRUYSWEG respectively – Billets in country farm houses widely scattered. All sanitary arrangements inadequate.	
"	6	–	Disinfection of billet C Coy 10th KOYLI where case of measles reported carried out. Negotiated with 126th Field Coy RE re carrying out necessary alterations at Salt Refinery WORMHOUDT to erect baths for 64th Bgde – To Corps HQ to interview C.E. re provision of complete spray bath sets.	
"	7	–	Work begun on 64th Bgde baths, WORMHOUDT. Geyser & cistern erected. Inspection of sanitation of 1st E.Yorks.	
"	8	–	Routine sanitary duties.	

WAR DIARY or INTELLIGENCE SUMMARY

Army Form C. 2118

Place	Date 1917. Feb.	Hour	Summary of Events and Information	Remarks and references to Appendices
Wormhoudt	10	-	Adjutant R.E. announces that no further supplies of material will be available in this area.	
	11	-	NCOs & men of section entrained at ESQUELBECQ for 1st Corps area. Details left behind to look after clothing. 600 cwt taken to POPERINGHE for 62nd Brigade.	
BETHUNE	12 & 13	-	Part of section – majority NCOs & men in BETHUNE, previous to entering 6th Div'l area.	
BETHUNE	14	-	Billets at SAILLY-LABOURSE taken over; 6th Div'l San Sec moved out under orders on 12th.	
SAILLY-LABOURSE	15	-	D.H.Q. remains at BETHUNE. Tour of inspection of SAILLY-LABOURSE & NOYELLES and two NCOs detailed for ANNEQUIN. 1 NCO to VERQUIGNEUL. Sanitary state of above very unsatisfactory. Latrines in many cases fouled, pits full to the top & above. Refuse & ordure left about uncollected – Apparently no supervision by previous Div'l San Sec, certainly little or nothing done towards efficient sanitation. Two bathhouses viz: LABOURSE & VERMELLES (brewery) out of action from burst pipes due to frost. C.R.E. advised to repair.	
"	16	-	Officers latrine in Londonderry Road, SAILLY, reerected over new pit. New trenches required in Gold Road & Derry Road and 3 in LABOURSE. Ground very hard from frost. Work of repair at LABOURSE bathhouse put in hand. 15 new lengths of piping required. 6th Div'l San Sec left 20 pipe lengths for this work.	
"	17	-	Continued pit digging & collection of refuse. The latter is so abundant that g.s. wagons will have to be requisitioned from 64th Field Ambulance (LABOURSE) to cope with it. Reports continue to be received from all quarters of filthy condition in which area was left by 6th Div.	

Wm Thurstone
Capt.

WAR DIARY or INTELLIGENCE SUMMARY

Army Form C. 2118

(Erase heading not required.)

Place	Date Feb. 1917	Hour	Summary of Events and Information	Remarks and references to Appendices
SAILLY-LABOURSE	18	-	Made tour of inspection of ANNEQUIN. Latrines in state of disrepair in Walker Road. 3-seater bucket latrine left without covers. Fresh canvas required to cover that in Walker Road. Lids removed in majority of cases presumably for firewood. Incinerators untidy. Burnt tins re unremoved to dumps. Baths have been used at ANNEQUIN for past two days. (9th & 10th HOYLI bathed)	
"	19	-	Sanitation of DHQ, Chateau Des Pres, SAILLY, taken over. Special report sent to A.D.M.S. detailing unsatisfactory nature of sanitation on moving into this area. 4 GS. wagons at work removing accumulation of refuse & tins. 2 carpenters sent to repair latrines at ANNEQUIN.	
"	20	-	To VERMELLES. Found drinking-water tank at Cross-roads VERMELLES unattended. Sent up San Sec man i/c forthwith to clean tank & chlorinate water for drinking. P.B. man wanted for incinerator behind brewery & GS wagon to collect refuse.	
"	21	-	1 NCO to trenches on water duty. Billet 109 disinfected. Case of German measles. Report from NCO at NOYELLES that sanitary state of this place is very unsatisfactory.	
"	22	-	Visited VERQUIN. Interviewed Capt Kilbride re case of C.S.M. Inspected billet 27 contacts. Billet of CSM case at VERQUIN disinfected & blankets "stoved" in San Sec Thresh. Diagnosis not confirmed. NCO left strength on railway duty to BOULOGNE.	
"	23	-	Inspection of NOEUX-LES-MINES, Divl Train (A&Companies) there. Report satisfactory. Visited trenches to take samples of water from OB5 & OB4. Character of water at OB4, well contaminated by Trench mud. Samples to be sent to No 6 Mob Lab. for analysis. R.E. communicated with to fit up pumps and tanks at OB.1 to remedy defects at OB.4.	

Wm T. Winstone Capt.

WAR DIARY or INTELLIGENCE SUMMARY

Army Form C. 2118

Instructions regarding War Diaries and Intelligence Summaries are contained in F.S. Regs., Part II. and the Staff Manual respectively. Title Pages will be prepared in manuscript.

(Erase heading not required.)

Place	Date	Hour	Summary of Events and Information	Remarks and references to Appendices
SAILLY-LABOURSE	Oct. 24 1917	—	Case of Scarlet Fever reported from 98th R.F. NOYELLES, billet disinfected in Chateau NOYELLES. Report of Sanitary improvements since entering this area drafted & sent to A.D.M.S.	
	25	—	All bathhouses visited to inspect efficiency in regard to viewing arrangements. Tin-tallies being made in duplicate to assist in having this efficiently carried out. NCO sent to inspect MAZINGARBE — Reports sanitation as affecting reserve battalion, 62nd Brigade satisfactory. Made complete tour of inspection of NOYELLES. Found sanitation slightly improved but collections of refuse so large that time will be necessary to clear.	
"	26	—	Repairs to urinals, latrines &c at NOYELLES carried out. Sanitary work somewhat impeded by Medical board on T.U.men. Bathhouses at LABOURSE, NOYELLES & VERMELLES visited. Women again employed as ovriers at LABOURSE which started bathing to-day.	
"	27	—	2 Carpenters & 5 fatigue men to VERMELLES to alter 3 latrines & execute repairs. Also carpenters finished work at NOYELLES. Made complete tour of inspection of LABOURSE. Certain minor defects require to be remedied. Another incinerator to be built at public incinerator yard.	
"	28	—	Inspected VERMELLES & NOYELLES in entirety. Much improvement noticeable with regard to cleanliness of area generally. Refuse is being collected & ground surface is clean. Incinerators are sufficient to burn all combustible refuse. Repairs recently executed on latrines have rendered them satisfactory. Examination of Cooker supplies & water carts continues. Report on samples of water sent to No 6 Mob Lab not yet received. One highly contaminated sample obtained in LABOURSE. Pump in 64th F.A. Yard. To be sent for analysis. Wm T Johnstone Capt.	

21st Div.   140/2043

March 1917

No. 38. Sanitary Section.

COMMITTEE FOR THE
MEDICAL HISTORY OF THE WAR
Date   11 MAY 1917

WAR DIARY / INTELLIGENCE SUMMARY

38 Sanitary Section
MEDICAL
Vol 19
Army Form C. 2118

Place	Date	Hour	Summary of Events and Information	Remarks and references to Appendices
SAILLY-LABOURSE	March 1	–	Medical examination of Section for classification into categories "A" & Lower categories. Latrine in Meynell Road, LABOURSE re-erected. 9th Suffolks (6th Div.) horse lines sprayed for manure disinfection. Incinerator at LABOURSE in course of construction. 62nd Bgde relieves in Cuinchy Sector. [by 71st Bgde 6th Div.]	
"	2	–	To 21st Divl Laundry, BETHUNE, then to ROBECQ & found 70th Works bathing. Interviewed Town Major, LILLERS re taking over baths at LILLERS after evacuation by 20th Div. To LABOUVRIERE to interview OC 20th Divl Composite Coy re starting bathing at LILLERS at 8 a.m. on Sunday morning. This was agreed to. 12th N.F. bathed at College de jeune fille baths, BETHUNE under arrangement 5th Div.	
"	3	–	Continued bathing at ROBECQ. Interviewed Staff Capt 62nd Bgde re concentrating all bathing at LILLERS instead of oddments at ROBECQ. 13th N.F. bathed at College jeune filles, BETHUNE.	
"	4	–	Relief of 64th Bgde in CAMBRIN SECTOR commences. Baths at ANNEQUIN handed over to 5th Div also service dress. Bathing begun at LILLERS this morning, baths taken over from 24th Div. – There can deal with 700 per diem.	
"	5	–	Case of measles notified in 64th Bgde Signals at HQ, ANNEQUIN. Necessary disinfection carried out. Visited Sani Sec workshop. Material in hand, 14 latrines complete & 8 urinals for eventualities. New incinerator at public incinerator yard nearly completed at LABOURSE.	
"	6	–	Medically examined men of Mob. Vet. Sec. for classification into categories. Arranged for bathing of same at College de jeune filles, BETHUNE. No definite information available from Camp Commandant re disposition of D.H.Q. & future movement. N.C.Os. returned from NOYELLES & VERMELLES.	
"	7	–	To VERMELLES, 110th Bgde baths & sock store. Wall of former hit with shell yesterday. No material damage done. Staff Capt 110th Bgde negotiates for supply of clothing to be left when Div moves – 2500 sets to be arranged for. To LILLERS & ROBECQ re arranging final bathing of 62nd & 64th Bgdes respectively.	

Wm Johnstone
Capt.

WAR DIARY or INTELLIGENCE SUMMARY

Army Form C. 2118

(Erase heading not required.)

Place	Date March	Hour	Summary of Events and Information	Remarks and references to Appendices
SAILLY-LABOURSE	8	—	To LILLERS & RIBECA re bathing arrangements. Deficiency of clothing at latter — Rectified by transfer of clothing from LILLERS. 200 sets. San Sec lorry cleared both bathhouses. Sanitation of SAILLY & LABOURSE satisfactory but work of refuse collecting hampered (withdrawal of I/3 wagons to 9th Res. Park under instructions 1st Corps.	
"	9	—	Latrine re-erected at D.H.Q. Lorry sent, after repair, with sanitary appliances and advance party to LUCHEUX.	
"	10	—	Disinfection carried out at billet 35 Holland St. VERMELLES — Case of German Measles reported. 6 NCOs & men to laundry i/c convoy of lorries to new area. Another lorry load with some men to LUCHEUX.	
"	11	—	Remainder of section left SAILLY-LABOURSE for LUCHEUX.	
LUCHEUX	12	—	Lorry reached LUCHEUX at 2 p.m. having been 24 hours on journey owing to state of roads. Case of German measles reported at billet 21 GROUCOTES. Diagnosis confirmed.	
"	13	—	General inspection of LUCHEUX. Village found very dirty. Much refuse, ordure & excreta everywhere. Latrine and incinerator accommodation inadequate. 286 (AT) RE do latrine construction for this area. — Baths in LUCHEUX at billet 223. — 6 sprays.	
"	14	—	Visited HALLOY and made general inspection. Latrines of 8-seater back to back type, with two 16-seaters of a similar type, screening only, no sheds. Most of them without lids & trenches not deep enough. Incinerators quite inadequate, & no proper tin dumps. 12th N.F. at C Camp; 13th N.F. & 1st Lines in billets in village.	
"	15	—	Inspected 64th Brigade area at LE SOUICH with Town Major. Sanitary arrangements practically nil. Scheme proposed by 30th Divn. San Sec but not carried out.	
"	16	—	Workshop established at LE SOUICH for area, including BREVILLERS & TVERGNY. New latrines erected in LUCHEUX and repairs to old ones. Interviewed Officer i/c CAGNY laundry. No washing can be undertaken for this Divn for a fortnight.	

WAR DIARY or INTELLIGENCE SUMMARY

Army Form C. 2118

Place	Date March	Hour	Summary of Events and Information	Remarks and references to Appendices
LUCHEUX	17	—	Inspected BREVILLERS in its entirety with Town Major LE SOUICH. But for a few trenches and a 5-seater bucket latrine at 63rd F.A. billet 6, an incinerator opposite this village is also devoid of sanitary appliances. These will be made at Section Workshop LE SOUICH. TO OPPY to see baths, 6 sprays here. Informed Staff Capt 168th Bgde, 56th Div, that they use these baths.	
"	18	—	Removal of refuse undertaken daily in LUCHEUX. Constructional work proceeding at LE SOUICH. 5 lorry loads of clothing brought to store, billet 114 LUCHEUX. BETHUNE laundry cleared of all clothing. Case of C.S.M. reported from Labour Batt. Nissen hut disinfected near billet 29 LUCHEUX.	
"	19	—	Made further inspection of HALLOY. C Camp appears cleaner, Destructors for refuse required. Arrangements made to send dirty disinfected clothing to C.O.O. PARIS for washing, pending provision of a Divl. laundry. 2000 articles put up in sacks ready to be despatched to railhead. Two seater Officers latrine at back of billet 25 & 3-seater men's near billet 23 erected at LE SOUICH.	
"	20	—	Inspected VIIth Corps reserve Camp BOUQUEMAISON with CO. Advised suitable sites for sanitary conveniences. Wired O.Yc no 8 Mob Lab to analyse water supply which is from a deep well.	
"	21	—	Inspected LUCHEUX in its entirety. Found considerable improvement, but sanitation of Rue & Brightly Roads could be improved. TO LE SOUICH to hasten progress of work there & interview Town Major re clearing of some very foul civilian middens, at billets 46, 45 & 39. Maire was interviewed re clearances.	
"	22	—	Routine sanitary inspections carried on. 2311 bathed at LUCHEUX during past week.	
"	23	—	LE SOUICH & BREVILLERS area taken over by 56th Divn. — 64th Bgde moved out to PONMERA & GROUAS.	
"	24	—	Workshop at LE SOUICH disbanded and N.C.O.s & carpenters brought back to HQ from LE SOUICH. Laundry for Divl. washing procured at 81 Rue Du Bourg, DOULLENS. Work to be begun on Monday.	Wm J ——— Capt.

WAR DIARY or INTELLIGENCE SUMMARY

Army Form C. 2118

(Erase heading not required.)

Instructions regarding War Diaries and Intelligence Summaries are contained in F. S. Regs., Part II. and the Staff Manual respectively. Title Pages will be prepared in manuscript.

Place	Date March	Hour	Summary of Events and Information	Remarks and references to Appendices
LUCHEUX	25	-	To BAVINCOURT to make preliminary arrangements about taking on Sanitary work there. Visited LA CAUCHIE and HUMBERCAMP with special reference to baths accommodation. Sprays (6) in each village. They are both very dirty.	
"	26	-	4000 articles taken to DOULLENS laundry for washing also 16 gallons of petrol as per authority from DDS&T that this should be supplied on repayment. 50 Litres per diem the maximum. Conference at School of Sanitation 3rd Army. Informed that San Secs would become army troops very shortly. Preliminary proposals re carrying on Sanitation in specified areas submitted.	
"	27	-	Biscuit tin incinerator built at LUCHEUX behind R.E. Yard, capable of burning 1 ton refuse per diem. Interviewed O.C. 58th San. Sec at BAVINCOURT re taking over on the following day.	
"	28	-	Personnel of San Sec marched to BAVINCOURT, except NCO i/c Clothing Store LUCHEUX. Foden thresh left behind at LUCHEUX owing to condition of roads & want of steam coal.	
BAVINCOURT	29	-	Inspected D.A.Q. Stables left with manure unremoved & large pile of tins near incinerator. General sanitary condition of village poor. Sanitary appliances in many cases require repair. Went to LAHERLIÈRE & interviewed Town Major re possibility of procuring a div. Clothing Store at billets 16.	
"	30	-	Officially informed that San Secs henceforward become army troops. No 38 to proceed to area no. 10. VIIth Corps with HQ at BELLACOURT on April 1st. Lieut Haines 'Q' office to be O.C. baths. Handed over Laundry agreement & statements of amount of Clothing in Store at LUCHEUX - about 12,000 sets altogether. Accounts & vouchers relating to BETHUNE Laundry handed in to balance imprest a/c.	
"	31	-	PAS, GRINCOURT & WARLINCOURT visited. Sanitation of PAS seems satisfactory no troops in GRINCOURT. Dispositions of NCOs & men to villages in new area drawn up. No 10 area VIIth Corps includes 16 villages. NCOs already in charge of PONNIER, BERLES-au-BOIS, LA CAUCHIE & HUMBERCAMP areas.	

Wm Johnstone Capt.
O.C. 38 Sanitary Section

www.ingramcontent.com/pod-product-compliance
Lightning Source LLC
Chambersburg PA
CBHW081239170426
43191CB00034B/1982